FAVORITE BRAND NAME

Quick Soups, Stews & Breads

PUBLICATIONS INTERNATIONAL, LTD.

Front cover photograph and photograph on page 7 by Sanders
Studios, Inc., Chicago, IL.

Pictured on the front cover: Sante Fe Stew Olé *(page 13)* and
Jalapeño-Bacon Corn Bread *(page 83)*.

Pictured on the back cover *(clockwise from top right):* Garden
Vegetable Muffins *(page 70)*, Beef Bourguignon *(page 6)*, Hearty
Chicken and Rice Soup *(page 38)* and Picante Onion Soup *(page 61)*.

ISBN: 0-7853-1313-3

8 7 6 5 4 3 2 1

> **Microwave ovens vary in wattage. The cooking times given in this
> publication are approximate. Use the cooking times as guidelines and
> check for doneness before adding more time. Consult manufacturer's
> instructions for suitable microwave-safe cooking dishes.**

FAVORITE BRAND NAME

Quick Soups, Stews & Breads

Memorable Meats

Whether you prefer beef, pork, lamb or veal, these mouthwatering soups and stews will answer your meal-time needs. Serve them with bread and salad to round out your meal.

Beef Bourguignon

- 1 boneless beef sirloin steak, ½ inch thick, trimmed, cut into ½-inch pieces (about 3 pounds)
- ½ cup all-purpose flour
- 4 slices bacon, diced
- 3 cups Burgundy wine or beef broth
- 2 medium carrots, diced
- 1 teaspoon dried marjoram leaves, crushed
- ½ teaspoon dried thyme leaves, crushed
- ½ teaspoon salt
  Pepper to taste
- 1 bay leaf
- 2 tablespoons vegetable oil
- 20 to 24 fresh pearl onions
- 8 small new red potatoes, cut into quarters
- 8 to 10 mushrooms, sliced
- 3 cloves garlic, minced

Coat beef with flour, shaking off excess. Set aside.

Cook and stir bacon in 5-quart Dutch oven over medium-high heat until partially cooked. Brown half of beef with bacon in Dutch oven over medium-high heat. Remove with slotted spoon; set aside. Brown remaining beef. Pour off drippings. Return beef and bacon to Dutch oven.

Stir in wine, carrots, marjoram, thyme, salt, pepper and bay leaf. Bring to a boil over high heat. Reduce heat to low. Cover and simmer 10 minutes.

Meanwhile, heat oil in large saucepan over medium-high heat. Cook and stir onions, potatoes, mushrooms and garlic about 10 minutes. Add to Dutch oven. Cover and simmer 50 minutes or until meat is fork-tender. Discard bay leaf before serving.

Makes 10 to 12 servings

Beef Bourguignon

Tasty Pork Ragoût

Tasty Pork Ragoût

½ pound pork loin, cubed
1 small onion, sliced
1 large clove garlic, pressed
½ teaspoon dried rosemary, crumbled
2 tablespoons margarine
  Salt and pepper
1 bouillon cube, any flavor
½ cup boiling water
2 cups DOLE® Cauliflower florettes
1 cup sliced DOLE® Carrots
1 cup hot cooked rice

• Brown pork with onion, garlic and rosemary in margarine. Season with salt and pepper to taste.

• Dissolve bouillon in water; stir into pork mixture. Cover; simmer 20 minutes.

• Add cauliflower and carrots. Cover; simmer 5 minutes longer or until tender-crisp. Serve with rice.
Makes 2 servings

Preparation time: 10 minutes
Cooking time: 25 minutes

Spanish Beef Stew

¼ cup olive oil, divided
1 medium onion, chopped
3 cloves garlic, chopped
1 beef round steak, ½ inch thick, trimmed, cut into ¼-inch pieces (about 2 pounds)
1 can (28 ounces) whole peeled tomatoes, undrained, coarsely chopped
2 sweet potatoes, quartered and sliced (about 1 pound)
1 can (10½ ounces) condensed beef broth
1 medium green bell pepper, cut into pieces
1 cup frozen kernel corn
3 tablespoons balsamic or red wine vinegar
½ teaspoon dried coriander leaves, crushed *or* 1½ teaspoons finely chopped fresh cilantro leaves*
¼ teaspoon ground red pepper *or* ½ teaspoon crushed red pepper flakes
2 tablespoons water
2 tablespoons cornstarch
  Hot cooked rice (optional)
  Chopped fresh cilantro for garnish

*When using fresh cilantro, add to stew during last 5 minutes of cooking.

Heat 1 tablespoon oil in 5-quart Dutch oven over medium-high heat. Cook and stir onion and garlic until onion is soft. Remove with slotted spoon; set aside.

(continued)

Brown half of beef in 2 tablespoons oil in Dutch oven over medium-high heat. Remove with slotted spoon; set aside. Brown remaining beef in remaining 1 tablespoon oil. Pour off drippings. Return beef, onion and garlic to Dutch oven.

Add tomatoes with liquid, sweet potatoes, broth, bell pepper, corn, vinegar, coriander and ground red pepper. Bring to a boil over high heat. Reduce heat to low. Cover and simmer 40 minutes.

Blend water into cornstarch in small cup until smooth. Stir into stew. Cook and stir until stew boils and sauce is slightly thickened. Serve over rice. Garnish with fresh cilantro.   *Makes 6 to 8 servings*

Veal Chili

2 tablespoons vegetable oil, divided
1½ cups chopped onions
3 cloves garlic, minced
2 pounds veal for stew, cut into ½-inch pieces
  Salt
2 cans (14½ ounces *each*) whole peeled tomatoes, undrained, coarsely chopped
  Water
2 tablespoons chili powder
1 tablespoon unsweetened cocoa
1 tablespoon ground cumin
1 can (15 ounces) black beans or kidney beans, drained

Heat 2 teaspoons oil in Dutch oven over medium heat. Cook onions and garlic until onions are soft, about 3 minutes. Remove from pan with slotted spoon; set aside.

Brown one-third veal in same Dutch oven over medium-high heat. Remove with slotted spoon; set aside. Brown remaining veal in two more batches, adding remaining oil as needed. Pour off drippings.

Return onion mixture and veal to Dutch oven. Season with salt. Stir in tomatoes with liquid (breaking up tomatoes with spoon) and enough water (about 1 cup) to cover ingredients.

Stir in chili powder, cocoa and cumin; bring to a boil over high heat. Reduce heat to low. Cover and simmer 45 minutes or until veal is fork-tender. Add beans; continue simmering, uncovered, about 10 minutes or until heated through.
Makes 8 servings

Preparation time: 30 minutes
Cooking time: 55 minutes

Favorite recipe from **National Live Stock & Meat Board**

Veal Chili

Canton Pork Stew

1½ pounds boneless lean pork
    shoulder or pork loin roast,
    cut into 1-inch pieces
1 teaspoon ground ginger
¼ teaspoon ground cinnamon
¼ teaspoon ground red pepper
1 tablespoon peanut or
    vegetable oil
1 large onion, coarsely chopped
3 cloves garlic, minced
1 can (about 14 ounces) chicken
    broth
¼ cup dry sherry
1 package (about 10 ounces)
    frozen baby carrots, thawed
1 large green bell pepper, cut
    into 1-inch pieces
3 tablespoons soy sauce
1½ tablespoons cornstarch
    Cilantro for garnish

Sprinkle pork with ginger,
cinnamon and ground red pepper;
toss well. Heat large saucepan or
Dutch oven over medium-high heat.
Add oil; heat until hot.

Add pork to saucepan; brown on all
sides. Add onion and garlic; cook
2 minutes, stirring frequently. Add
broth and sherry. Bring to a boil
over high heat. Reduce heat to
medium-low. Cover and simmer
40 minutes.

Stir in carrots and green pepper;
cover and simmer 10 minutes or
until pork is fork-tender. Blend soy
sauce into cornstarch in cup until
smooth. Stir into stew. Cook and stir
1 minute or until stew boils and
thickens. Ladle into soup bowls.
Garnish with cilantro.
Makes 6 servings

Mexican Vegetable Beef Soup

1 pound lean ground beef
½ cup chopped onion
1 package (1.25 ounces)
    LAWRY'S® Taco Spices &
    Seasonings
1 can (28 ounces) whole
    tomatoes, undrained and
    cut up
1 package (16 ounces) frozen
    mixed vegetables, thawed
1 can (15 ounces) kidney beans,
    undrained
1 can (14½ ounces) beef broth

In Dutch oven, brown ground beef
and onion, stirring until beef is
cooked through; drain fat. Add Taco
Spices & Seasonings, tomatoes,
vegetables, beans and broth. Bring
to a boil; reduce heat and simmer,
uncovered, 5 minutes, stirring
occasionally. *Makes 6 servings*

Presentation: Top each serving with
corn chips and grated Cheddar
cheese.

Hint: For extra flavor, add chopped
cilantro to beef mixture.

Canton Pork Stew

Patrick's Irish Lamb Soup

1½ pounds fresh lean American lamb boneless shoulder, cut into ¾-inch cubes
1 tablespoon olive oil
1 medium onion, coarsely chopped
1 bottle (12 ounces) beer *or* ¾ cup water
1 teaspoon seasoned pepper
2 cans (14.5 ounces *each*) beef or chicken broth
1 package (.87 ounces) brown gravy mix
3 cups cubed new potatoes
2 cups thinly sliced carrots
2 cups shredded green cabbage
Chopped parsley for garnish

Heat oil in 3-quart saucepan over medium-high heat. Cook and stir lamb and onion in oil until lamb is brown and onion is soft. Stir in beer and pepper. Bring to a boil over high heat. Reduce heat to low. Cover and simmer 30 minutes.

Stir in broth and gravy mix. Add potatoes and carrots; cover and simmer 15 to 20 minutes until lamb and vegetables are fork-tender. Stir in cabbage; cook just until cabbage turns bright green. Garnish with chopped parsley.

Makes 8 servings

Favorite recipe from **American Lamb Council**

Patrick's Irish Lamb Soup

Vermont Vegetable Stew

1 pound ECKRICH® Smoked Sausage, sliced thin
1 medium onion, chopped
1 tablespoon vegetable oil
1 can (28 ounces) whole tomatoes, undrained, cut up
3 cups water
1 can (15 ounces) red kidney beans, undrained
1 can (8 ounces) tomato sauce
¼ head green cabbage, cut into 1-inch pieces
3 ribs celery, sliced
3 carrots, sliced
2 tablespoons uncooked rice
2 teaspoons beef bouillon granules
1 bay leaf
½ teaspoon dried thyme leaves

Sauté onion in oil in Dutch oven until tender. Add remaining ingredients. Bring to a boil over high heat. Reduce heat to low; cover and simmer 30 minutes or until vegetables are tender. Remove bay leaf before serving.

Makes 8 servings

Left to right: Jalapeño-Bacon Corn Bread (page 83) and Santa Fe Stew Olé

Santa Fe Stew Olé

  1 tablespoon vegetable oil
1½ pounds beef stew meat, cut
     into bite-size pieces
  1 can (28 ounces) stewed
     tomatoes
  2 medium carrots, cut into
     ¼-inch slices
  1 medium onion, coarsely
     chopped
  1 package (1.25 ounces)
     LAWRY'S® Taco Spices &
     Seasonings
  2 tablespoons diced green chiles
  ½ teaspoon LAWRY'S® Seasoned
     Salt
  ¼ cup water
  2 tablespoons all-purpose flour
  1 can (15 ounces) pinto beans,
     drained

In Dutch oven, heat oil, then brown stew meat. Add tomatoes, carrots, onion, Taco Spices & Seasonings, green chiles and Seasoned Salt; blend well. Bring to a boil; reduce heat. Cover and simmer 40 minutes. In small bowl, combine water and flour; blend well. Stir into stew mixture. Add pinto beans; simmer an additional 15 minutes.

Makes 4 servings

Beef and Bean Soup with Pesto

Beef and Bean Soup with Pesto

- **1 pound beef strips for stir-fry***
- **2 teaspoons olive oil**
- **1 can (28 ounces) plum tomatoes, broken up**
- **1 cup ready-to-serve beef broth Pesto Sauce (recipe follows)**
- **1 can (15 ounces) Great Northern beans, drained**

*For stir-fry beef strips, cut 1-inch-thick beef sirloin or top round steak into ⅛- or ¼-inch-thick strips.

Cut beef strips for stir-fry into 1-inch pieces. Heat oil in Dutch oven or large saucepan over medium heat. Brown half of beef. Remove with slotted spoon; set aside. Brown remaining beef. Pour off drippings, if necessary.

Stir in tomatoes, beef broth and reserved beef. Bring to a boil over high heat. Reduce heat to low. Cover and simmer, stirring occasionally, 35 to 40 minutes until beef is fork-tender.

Meanwhile, prepare Pesto Sauce; reserve. Add beans to beef mixture; heat through. Serve with Pesto Sauce. *Makes 4 servings*

Preparation time: 5 minutes
Cooking time: 50 minutes

PESTO SAUCE: Place ½ cup parsley sprigs (stems removed), ¼ cup grated Parmesan cheese and 1 to 2 cloves garlic in blender or food processor container; cover and process until finely chopped. Add 2 tablespoons olive oil; process until paste forms. Set aside.

Favorite recipe from **National Live Stock & Meat Board**

Bistro Beef Soup

1 pound boneless beef top sirloin steak, 1 inch thick
1 large onion, cut into quarters
2 tablespoons olive oil, divided
½ teaspoon coarsely ground black pepper
¾ pound potatoes, peeled, cut into ½-inch pieces
½ pound carrots, cut into ¼-inch slices
3 cups ready-to-serve beef broth
1 tablespoon *each* dried chives, crushed dried parsley, chervil and basil leaves
½ teaspoon salt
2 tablespoons red wine vinegar

Cut steak into 1 × ½-inch strips. Cut two onion quarters crosswise into thin slices. Chop remaining onion; reserve. Combine beef with sliced onion, 1 tablespoon oil and pepper; refrigerate.

Heat remaining 1 tablespoon oil in large saucepan over medium-low heat until hot. Add chopped onion, potatoes and carrots. Cover tightly; cook 10 minutes, stirring occasionally.

Add beef broth, chives, parsley, chervil and basil leaves. Bring to a boil over high heat. Reduce heat to low. Simmer, uncovered, 10 minutes or until vegetables are fork-tender.

Meanwhile, heat large nonstick skillet over high heat. Stir-fry beef and onion (half at a time) 2 to 3 minutes; season with salt. Remove meat with slotted spoon; reserve. Add vinegar; heat and stir to loosen browned meat on bottom of skillet. Stir into broth mixture. To serve, place equal amounts of beef mixture into four soup bowls; pour broth mixture over beef. Serve immediately. *Makes 4 servings*

Preparation time: 20 minutes
Cooking time: 25 minutes

Favorite recipe from **National Live Stock & Meat Board**

Texas Fajita Chili

1¼ cups chopped onion
1 cup chopped green bell pepper
1 tablespoon vegetable oil
2 cans (15 ounces *each*) kidney beans, drained
1 pound shredded, cooked pork or beef
1 can (14½ ounces) whole peeled tomatoes, undrained and cut up
1 cup LAWRY'S® Fajitas Skillet Sauce
1 can (7 ounces) whole kernel corn, drained
½ cup tomato juice or beer
1½ teaspoons chili powder

In large skillet, sauté onion and bell pepper in oil 10 minutes or until tender. Stir in kidney beans, shredded meat, tomatoes, Fajitas Skillet Sauce, corn, tomato juice and chili powder. Bring mixture to a boil. Reduce heat; cover and simmer 20 minutes. *Makes 6 servings*

Presentation: Serve in individual bowls topped with grated Monterey Jack cheese or sour cream. If desired, serve with dash of hot pepper sauce.

Chili à la Mexico

2 pounds ground beef
2 cups finely chopped onions
2 cloves garlic, minced
1 can (28 ounces) whole peeled
    tomatoes, undrained,
    coarsely chopped
1 can (6 ounces) tomato paste
1½ to 2 tablespoons chili powder
1 teaspoon ground cumin
¼ teaspoon salt
¼ teaspoon ground red pepper
    (optional)
¼ teaspoon ground cloves
    (optional)
    Lime wedges and cilantro
    sprigs for garnish

Brown beef in deep 12-inch skillet
over medium-high heat 6 to 8
minutes, stirring to separate meat.
Reduce heat to medium. Pour off
drippings. Add onions and garlic;
cook and stir 5 minutes or until
onions are softened.

Stir in tomatoes, tomato paste, chili
powder, cumin, salt, red pepper and
cloves. Bring to a boil over high
heat. Reduce heat to low. Cover and
simmer 30 minutes, stirring
occasionally. Ladle into bowls.
Garnish with lime wedges and
cilantro.   *Makes 6 to 8 servings*

Hungarian Beef Stew

¼ cup vegetable oil
1 medium onion, chopped
1 cup sliced mushrooms
2 teaspoons paprika
1 boneless beef sirloin steak,
    ½ inch thick, trimmed, cut
    into ½-inch pieces (about
    2 pounds)
½ cup beef broth
½ teaspoon caraway seeds
    Salt and pepper to taste
2 tablespoons all-purpose flour
1 cup sour cream
    Hot buttered noodles
    (optional)
    Chopped parsley for garnish

Heat oil in 5-quart Dutch oven over
medium-high heat. Cook and stir
onion and mushrooms in oil until
onion is soft. Stir in paprika.
Remove with slotted spoon; set
aside.

Brown half of beef in Dutch oven
over medium-high heat. Remove
with slotted spoon; set aside. Brown
remaining beef. Pour off drippings.
Return beef, onion and mushrooms
to Dutch oven. Stir in broth,
caraway seeds, salt and pepper.
Bring to a boil over high heat.
Reduce heat to low. Cover and
simmer 45 minutes or until beef is
fork-tender.

Whisk flour into sour cream in
small bowl. Whisk into stew. Stir
until slightly thickened. *Do not boil.*
Serve over noodles. Garnish with
parsley.   *Makes 6 to 8 servings*

Chili à la Mexico

Hearty Beef Stew with Noodles

Hearty Beef Stew with Noodles

2 tablespoons vegetable oil
1 teaspoon finely chopped garlic
1 pound boneless beef sirloin steak, cut into ½-inch cubes
3 cups water
½ cup dry red wine
4 medium new potatoes, quartered
1 large carrot, thinly sliced
1 cup sliced mushrooms
1 cup sliced celery
1 large onion, cut into eighths
1 tablespoon tomato paste
¼ teaspoon dried thyme leaves
1 bay leaf
1 package LIPTON® Noodles & Sauce — Beef Flavor
1 tablespoon finely chopped parsley
Salt and pepper to taste

In 3-quart saucepan, heat oil and cook garlic over medium heat 30 seconds. Add beef and cook over medium heat, stirring frequently, 2 minutes or until browned. Stir in water, wine, potatoes, carrot, mushrooms, celery, onion, tomato paste, thyme and bay leaf. Bring to a boil, then simmer, stirring occasionally, 30 minutes or until beef is almost tender. Stir in noodles & beef flavor sauce and cook 10 minutes or until noodles are tender. Stir in parsley, salt and pepper. Remove bay leaf.

Makes about 4 (2-cup) servings

Pork with Apricots, Apple and Prunes

½ cup all-purpose flour
3 tablespoons dark brown sugar
1 pork tenderloin, cut into ½-inch cubes (about 2½ pounds)
¼ cup vegetable oil
1 large onion, thinly sliced
2 cloves garlic, minced
1½ cups apple juice
1 cup chicken broth
2 tablespoons Dijon-style mustard
1 tablespoon cider vinegar
1 Granny Smith apple, peeled and diced
1 cup chopped dried apricots
½ cup chopped pitted prunes
⅛ teaspoon ground cloves
Pepper to taste

Combine flour and brown sugar in shallow dish. Coat pork with flour mixture, shaking off excess. Heat oil in 5-quart Dutch oven over medium-high heat. Brown half of pork in Dutch oven. Remove with slotted spoon; set aside. Repeat with remaining pork.

Add onion and garlic to Dutch oven. Cook and stir 5 minutes or until onion is soft. Return pork to Dutch

(continued)

oven. Add apple juice, broth, mustard, vinegar, apple, apricots, prunes, cloves and pepper. Bring to a boil over high heat. Reduce heat to low. Cover and simmer 45 minutes or until pork is fork-tender and sauce is thickened.

Makes 6 to 8 servings

Beef Burgundy Stew

1 pound sirloin beef, cut into 1½-inch cubes
3 tablespoons all-purpose flour
6 slices bacon, cut into 1-inch pieces (about ¼ pound)
1 large onion, cut into wedges (about 1½ cups)
2 cloves garlic, crushed
3 carrots, cut into ½-inch pieces (about 1½ cups)
12 small mushrooms
1 cup Burgundy or other dry red wine
½ cup A.1.® Steak Sauce

Coat beef with flour; set aside. In large heavy pot, over medium heat, cook bacon until crisp; remove with slotted spoon and reserve. Brown beef, a few pieces at a time, in drippings. Return cooked beef and bacon to pot with onion, garlic, carrots, mushrooms, wine and steak sauce; cover. Simmer 40 minutes or until carrots are tender, stirring occasionally. *Makes 6 servings*

Preparation time: 15 minutes
Total time: 1 hour 10 minutes

Greek Pork Stew

¼ cup olive oil
1 pork tenderloin, cut into ½-inch cubes (about 2½ pounds)
½ pound small white onions, cut into halves
3 cloves garlic, chopped
1¼ cups dry red wine
1 can (6 ounces) tomato paste
1 can (14½ ounces) ready-to-serve beef broth
2 tablespoons balsamic vinegar or red wine vinegar
2 bay leaves
1½ teaspoons ground cinnamon
⅛ teaspoon ground coriander
Hot cooked rice (optional)

Heat oil in 5-quart Dutch oven over medium-high heat. Brown half of pork in Dutch oven. Remove with slotted spoon; set aside. Brown remaining pork. Remove with slotted spoon; set aside.

Add onions and garlic to Dutch oven. Cook and stir about 5 minutes or until onions are soft. Return pork to Dutch oven.

Combine wine and tomato paste in small bowl until blended; add to pork. Stir in broth, vinegar, bay leaves, cinnamon and coriander. Bring to a boil over high heat. Reduce heat to low. Cover and simmer 45 minutes or until pork is fork-tender. Remove bay leaves before serving. Serve with rice.

Makes 6 to 8 servings

Lentil and Sausage Ragoût

1 pound ECKRICH® Beef Smoked Sausage, cut into ¼-inch slices
2 large onions, sliced
3 tablespoons vegetable oil
3 cans (14½ ounces *each*) stewed tomatoes
2 large cloves garlic, minced
1½ teaspoons paprika
1 teaspoon dried thyme leaves
1 teaspoon dried marjoram leaves
Dash ground black pepper
1 cup lentils, sorted, rinsed
2 ribs celery, chopped
2 cups water
¼ cup chopped fresh parsley (optional)

Sauté onions in oil in large saucepan over medium heat until lightly browned. Add tomatoes with juice, garlic, paprika, thyme, marjoram and pepper. Bring to a boil over high heat. Reduce heat to low; simmer 10 minutes. Add sausage to tomato mixture; simmer 20 minutes more. Meanwhile, bring lentils and celery in water to a boil over high heat in separate saucepan. Reduce heat to low; cover and simmer 20 minutes or until lentils are tender. Drain; add to tomato mixture. Heat until hot. Garnish with parsley.

Makes 8 to 10 servings

Frank and Vegetable Soup

1 package (16 ounces) ECKRICH® Franks, cut into ¼-inch slices
1½ cups chopped onions
1 cup sliced carrots
½ cup sliced celery
1 tablespoon butter or margarine
1 can (14½ ounces) whole tomatoes, undrained
1 package (10 ounces) frozen cut green beans, thawed
5 cups beef broth or bouillon
Grated Parmesan cheese

Sauté onions, carrots and celery in butter in large saucepan over medium heat 5 minutes. Add tomatoes with juice; break up tomatoes. Mix in beans and broth. Bring to a boil over high heat. Reduce heat to low; simmer 15 minutes. Add franks; simmer 5 minutes more. Top each serving with cheese.   *Makes 8 servings*

Speedy Beef Soup

1 pound thin-cut beef tip steaks, cut into 4×½-inch strips
5 cups ready-to-serve beef broth
½ cup uncooked rotelle or wheel-shaped pasta
½ teaspoon salt
2 cups frozen mixed vegetables

Bring broth to a boil in Dutch oven over high heat. Add pasta and salt; return to a boil. Reduce heat to low. Cover and simmer 5 minutes. Add vegetables and return to a boil over

(continued)

high heat. Reduce heat to low. Cover and simmer 5 minutes or until pasta and vegetables are tender. Remove from heat. Add thin-cut beef tip steaks. Cover; let stand 5 minutes.

Makes 4 servings

Preparation time: 5 minutes
Cooking time: 12 minutes
Standing time: 5 minutes

Favorite recipe from **National Live Stock & Meat Board**

Chilly Day Chili

2 medium onions, chopped
1 green bell pepper, chopped
2 tablespoons vegetable oil
2 pounds lean ground beef
1 can (16 ounces) whole peeled tomatoes, undrained and cut into bite-size pieces
1 can (15 ounces) tomato sauce
½ cup HEINZ® Tomato Ketchup
1 to 2 tablespoons chili powder
1 teaspoon salt
¼ teaspoon pepper
2 cans (15 ounces *each*) red kidney beans, partially drained

In large saucepot or Dutch oven, sauté onions and green pepper in oil until tender-crisp. Add beef; cook until beef is browned, stirring occasionally. Drain excess fat. Add tomatoes, tomato sauce, ketchup, chili powder, salt and pepper. Simmer, uncovered, 30 minutes, stirring occasionally. Add kidney beans; simmer, uncovered, an additional 15 minutes.
Makes 10 servings (about 10 cups)

Lamb and Yam Stew

1 tablespoon finely chopped hot chile pepper
½ teaspoon ground black pepper
3 cloves garlic, minced
½ teaspoon ground cinnamon
1½ pounds boneless lamb, trimmed of excess fat and cut into 1-inch cubes
2 tablespoons FLEISCHMANN'S® Margarine
1 cup chopped onion
3 medium tomatoes, peeled, seeded and chopped
3 tablespoons no-salt-added tomato paste
1 pound yams or sweet potatoes, peeled and sliced
1 (13¾-ounce) can COLLEGE INN® Lower Salt Chicken Broth
4 cups hot cooked rice, prepared without salt

In small bowl, combine chile pepper, ground pepper, garlic and cinnamon. Rub mixture into lamb. In large heavy saucepan, over medium heat, brown lamb in margarine in small batches; remove from saucepan.

In same saucepan, sauté onion until tender. Add tomatoes and tomato paste; cook for 3 minutes. Add lamb, yams or sweet potatoes and broth. Cook, uncovered, for 30 minutes or until tender. Serve with rice.   *Makes 8 servings*

Wonton Soup

¼ **pound ground pork, chicken or turkey**
¼ **cup finely chopped water chestnuts**
2 **tablespoons soy sauce, divided**
1 **egg white, slightly beaten**
1 **teaspoon minced fresh ginger**
12 **wonton wrappers**
1 **can (46 ounces) chicken broth**
1½ **cups sliced fresh spinach leaves**
1 **cup thinly sliced cooked pork (optional)**
½ **cup diagonally sliced green onions**
1 **tablespoon Oriental sesame oil Shredded carrot for garnish**

Combine ground pork, water chestnuts, 1 tablespoon soy sauce, egg white and ginger in small bowl; mix well.

Place 1 wonton wrapper with a point toward edge of counter. Mound 1 teaspoon of filling toward bottom point. Fold bottom point over filling, then roll wrapper over once. Moisten inside points with water. Bring side points together below the filling, overlapping sightly; press together firmly to seal. Repeat with remaining wrappers and filling.* Keep finished wontons covered with plastic wrap, while filling remaining wrappers.

Combine broth and remaining 1 tablespoon soy sauce in large saucepan. Bring to a boil over high heat. Reduce heat to medium; add wontons. Simmer, uncovered, 4 minutes.

Stir in spinach, cooked pork and onions; remove from heat. Stir in sesame oil. Ladle into soup bowls. Garnish with shredded carrot.

Makes 2 servings

*Wontons may be made ahead to this point; cover and refrigerate up to 8 hours or freeze up to 3 months. Proceed as directed, if using refrigerated wontons. Increase simmer time to 6 minutes, if using frozen wontons.

Piedmont Pork Stew

1 **pound boneless pork loin, cut into 1-inch cubes**
1 **tablespoon vegetable oil**
8 **ounces mushrooms, chopped**
2 **carrots, sliced**
1 **medium onion, coarsely chopped**
1 **can (8 ounces) tomato sauce**
1 **cup dry red wine**
1 **teaspoon dried thyme leaves**
1 **teaspoon dried oregano leaves**
¼ **teaspoon ground cinnamon**
¼ **teaspoon salt**
½ **cup raisins Hot cooked rice or orzo**

Brown pork in oil in large pot over medium-high heat until browned, about 3 minutes. Stir in vegetables; cook and stir 2 minutes more.

Add tomato sauce, wine and seasonings. Bring to a boil over high heat. Reduce heat to low. Cover and simmer 15 to 20 minutes. Stir in raisins; heat through. Serve over rice. *Makes 6 servings*

Favorite recipe from **National Pork Producers Council**

Clockwise from top right: Wonton Soup, Easy Wonton Chips (page 80) and Beef Soup with Noodles (page 24)

Beef Soup with Noodles

2 tablespoons soy sauce
1 teaspoon minced fresh ginger
¼ teaspoon crushed red pepper flakes
1 boneless beef top sirloin steak, cut 1 inch thick (about ¾ pound)
1 tablespoon peanut or vegetable oil
2 cups sliced fresh mushrooms
2 cans (about 14 ounces *each*) beef broth
3 ounces (1 cup) fresh snow peas, cut diagonally into 1-inch pieces
1½ cups hot cooked fine egg noodles (2 ounces uncooked)
1 green onion, cut diagonally into thin slices
1 teaspoon Oriental sesame oil (optional)
    Red bell pepper strips for garnish
    Easy Wonton Chips (recipe page 80) (optional)

Combine soy sauce, ginger and pepper flakes in small bowl. Spread mixture evenly over both sides of steak. Marinate on plate at room temperature 15 minutes.

Heat deep skillet over medium-high heat. Add peanut oil; heat until hot. Drain steak; reserve soy sauce mixture (there will only be a small amount of mixture). Add steak to skillet; cook 4 to 5 minutes per side.* Let stand on cutting board 10 minutes.

Add mushrooms to skillet; stir-fry 2 minutes. Add broth, snow peas and reserved soy sauce mixture; bring to a boil, scraping up browned meat bits. Reduce heat to medium-low. Stir in noodles.

Cut steak across the grain into ⅛-inch slices; cut each slice into 1-inch pieces. Stir into soup; heat through. Stir in onion and sesame oil. Ladle into soup bowls. Garnish with red pepper strips. Serve with Easy Wonton Chips.

Makes 4 to 6 servings

*Cooking time is for medium-rare doneness. Adjust time for desired doneness.

Chunky Ham Stew

1 medium onion, chopped
2 ribs celery, sliced
2 carrots, sliced
4 cups low-sodium chicken broth
2 cups (8 ounces) ARMOUR® Lower Salt Ham, cut into ½-inch cubes
1 tablespoon MRS. DASH®, Original Blend
1 cup frozen peas
¼ cup water
2 tablespoons cornstarch

Combine onion, celery, carrots, broth, ham and seasoning in Dutch oven. Cover and cook over medium-high heat for 20 minutes, or until carrots are almost tender. Stir in peas. Mix water and cornstarch; add to stew. Stir constantly until stew comes to a boil and thickens. If desired, garnish with celery leaves.

Makes 4 to 6 servings

Ranch Clam Chowder

Ranch Clam Chowder

¼ cup chopped onion
3 tablespoons butter or margarine
½ pound fresh mushrooms, sliced
2 tablespoons Worcestershire sauce
1½ cups half-and-half
1 can (10¾ ounces) cream of potato soup
¼ cup dry white wine
1 package (1 ounce) **HIDDEN VALLEY RANCH®** Milk Recipe Original Ranch® Salad Dressing Mix
1 can (10 ounces) whole baby clams, undrained
Chopped parsley

In 3-quart saucepan, cook onion in butter over medium heat until onion is soft but not browned. Add mushrooms and Worcestershire sauce. Cook until mushrooms are soft and pan juices have almost evaporated. In medium bowl, whisk together half-and-half, potato soup, wine and salad dressing mix until smooth. Drain clam liquid into dressing mixture; stir into mushrooms in pan. Cook, uncovered, until soup is heated through but not boiling. Add clams to soup; cook until heated through. Garnish each serving with parsley.

Makes 6 servings

Seafood Gumbo

½ cup chopped onion
½ cup chopped green pepper
½ cup (about 2 ounces) sliced
  fresh mushrooms
1 clove garlic, minced
2 tablespoons margarine
1 can (28 ounces) whole
  tomatoes, undrained
2 cups chicken broth
½ to ¾ teaspoon ground red
  pepper
½ teaspoon dried thyme leaves
½ teaspoon dried basil leaves
1 package (10 ounces) frozen cut
  okra, thawed
¾ pound white fish, cut into
  1-inch pieces
½ pound peeled, deveined
  shrimp
3 cups hot cooked rice

Cook onion, green pepper, mushrooms, and garlic in margarine in large saucepan or Dutch oven over medium-high heat until tender-crisp. Stir in tomatoes and juice, broth, red pepper, thyme, and basil. Bring to a boil. Reduce heat; simmer, uncovered, 10 to 15 minutes. Stir in okra, fish, and shrimp; simmer until fish flakes with fork, 5 to 8 minutes. Serve rice on top of gumbo.

Makes 6 servings

Favorite recipe from **USA Rice Council**

New England Fish Chowder

¼ pound bacon, diced
1 cup chopped onion
½ cup chopped celery
2 cups diced russet potatoes
2 tablespoons all-purpose flour
2 cups water
1 bay leaf
1 teaspoon dried dill weed,
  crushed
1 teaspoon salt
½ teaspoon dried thyme leaves,
  crushed
½ teaspoon pepper
1 pound cod, haddock or halibut
  fillets, skinned, boned and
  cut into 1-inch pieces
2 cups milk or half-and-half
  Chopped parsley (optional)

Cook bacon in 5-quart Dutch oven over medium-high heat, stirring occasionally. Remove with slotted spoon; drain on paper towels. Add onion and celery to drippings. Cook and stir until onion is soft. Stir in potatoes; cook 1 minute. Stir in flour; cook 1 minute more.

Add water, bay leaf, dill weed, salt, thyme and pepper. Bring to a boil over high heat. Reduce heat to low. Cover and simmer 25 minutes or until potatoes are fork-tender. Add fish; simmer, covered, 5 minutes or until fish begins to flake when tested with a fork. Discard bay leaf. Return bacon to chowder. Add milk; heat through. *Do not boil.* Ladle into soup bowls. Garnish with parsley.

Makes 4 to 6 servings

Seafood Gumbo

Tuna Chowder

Tuna Chowder

- 1 pound yellowfin tuna steaks, skinned and cubed
- 1 can (10¾ ounces) low-sodium chicken broth
- 1 soup can water
- 1 cup diced potatoes
- ½ cup *each* chopped onion, carrots and celery
- ½ cup frozen corn
- ½ teaspoon dried basil
- ¼ teaspoon dried thyme
- ½ cup low-fat milk
- 1 tablespoon chopped parsley

Mix broth with 1 can of water in large saucepan; add potatoes. Bring to a boil over high heat. Reduce heat to low. Cover and simmer 10 to 15 minutes until potatoes are fork-tender.

Remove cooked potatoes from broth, reserving liquid. Purée cooked potatoes with ¼ cup broth.

Add tuna, vegetables, seasonings and puréed potatoes to remaining broth in saucepan. Cover; heat to simmering. Simmer 8 to 10 minutes until fish flakes easily when tested with a fork.

Stir in milk. Heat to serving temperature; *do not boil.* Sprinkle with parsley just before serving.

Makes 4 servings

Favorite recipe from **National Fisheries Institute**

Savory Seafood Soup

- 2½ cups water or chicken broth
- 1½ cups dry white wine
- 1 small onion, chopped
- ½ red bell pepper, chopped
- ½ green bell pepper, chopped
- 1 small clove garlic, minced
- ½ pound halibut, cut into 1-inch chunks
- ½ pound sea scallops, cut into halves
- 1 teaspoon dried thyme leaves, crushed
  Juice of ½ lime
  Dash of hot pepper sauce
  Salt and ground black pepper

Combine water, wine, onion, red and green peppers and garlic in large saucepan. Bring to a boil. Reduce heat to medium. Cover; simmer 15 minutes or until peppers are tender, stirring occasionally.

Add fish, scallops and thyme. Continue cooking 2 minutes or until fish and scallops turn opaque. Stir in lime juice and hot pepper sauce. Season with salt and black pepper to taste.

Makes 4 servings

Manhattan Clam Chowder

¼ cup chopped bacon
1 cup chopped onion
½ cup chopped carrots
½ cup chopped celery
3½ cups (28-ounce can)
    CONTADINA® Whole Peeled
    Tomatoes and juice
1 cup (8-ounce can)
    CONTADINA® Tomato Sauce
1 cup (8-ounce bottle) clam juice
1 large bay leaf
½ teaspoon chopped fresh
    rosemary
⅛ teaspoon pepper
1½ cups (two 6½-ounce cans)
    chopped clams and juice

Sauté bacon with onion, carrots and celery in large saucepan. Cut up tomatoes; stir in tomatoes and juice with remaining ingredients, except clams. Heat to boiling. Reduce heat; boil gently 15 minutes. Stir in clams and juice. Heat additional 5 minutes. Remove bay leaf before serving.   *Makes 6½ cups*

MICROWAVE DIRECTIONS:
Combine bacon, onion, carrots and celery in 2-quart microwave-safe casserole dish. Microwave on **HIGH** (100%) power for 5 minutes. Stir in remaining ingredients, except clams. Microwave on **HIGH** (100%) power for 5 minutes. Stir in clams and juice. Microwave on **HIGH** (100%) power for 5 minutes. Remove bay leaf before serving.

Spicy Crab Soup

1 pound crabmeat,* cooked,
    flaked and cartilage removed
1 can (28 ounces) crushed
    tomatoes in tomato purée,
    undrained
2 cups water
1 can (10¾ ounces) low-sodium
    chicken broth
¾ cup chopped celery
¾ cup diced onion
1 teaspoon seafood seasoning
¼ teaspoon lemon-pepper
1 package (10 ounces) frozen
    corn, thawed
1 package (10 ounces) frozen
    peas, thawed

*Purchase flake-style or a mixture of flake and chunk crabmeat if purchasing blue crab or surimi blended seafood.

Combine tomatoes, water, broth, celery, onion, seafood seasoning and lemon-pepper in 6-quart soup pot. Bring to a boil over high heat. Reduce heat to low. Cover and simmer 20 to 30 minutes. Add corn and peas; simmer 10 minutes more. Add crabmeat; simmer until hot.
            Makes 6 servings

Favorite recipe from **National Fisheries Institute**

Spicy Crab Soup

Seafood Niçoise

2 tablespoons olive oil
1 leek, white only, sliced (1 cup)
2 shallots, chopped
6 to 8 small red potatoes, cut
 into quarters
1 can (15 ounces) tomato purée
1 to 1½ cups bottled clam juice,
 divided
1 teaspoon salt
1 teaspoon herbes de Provence,
 crushed*
¼ teaspoon dried tarragon
 leaves, crushed
1 pound sea scallops or tuna, cut
 into 1-inch pieces
½ cup sliced pitted ripe olives
½ cup frozen French-cut string
 beans (optional)

*Substitute ¼ teaspoon *each* rubbed
sage, crushed dried rosemary,
thyme, oregano, marjoram and basil
leaves.

Heat oil in 5-quart Dutch oven over
medium-high heat. Cook and stir
leek and shallots in hot oil until soft.
Add potatoes; cook 10 minutes,
stirring occasionally. Stir in tomato
purée, 1 cup clam juice, salt and
herbs. Bring to a boil over high heat.
Reduce heat to low. Cover and
simmer 40 minutes or until potatoes
are fork-tender.

If sauce is too thick, add remaining
½ cup clam juice. Add scallops,
olives and beans. Cover and simmer
5 to 6 minutes until scallops are
opaque.   *Makes 4 servings*

Pescado Viejo
(Fish Stew)

2 medium onions, chopped
1 green bell pepper, diced
1 tablespoon vegetable oil
2 cans (14½ ounces *each*) whole
 peeled tomatoes, undrained
 and cut up
1 large red potato, cubed
1 can (13¾ ounces) beef broth
⅓ cup red wine
1 bay leaf
1 package (1.5 ounces)
 LAWRY'S® Original Style
 Spaghetti Sauce Spices &
 Seasonings
¾ teaspoon LAWRY'S® Garlic
 Powder with Parsley
½ teaspoon LAWRY'S® Seasoned
 Salt
½ teaspoon celery seed
1 pound halibut or swordfish
 steaks, rinsed and cubed

In Dutch oven, sauté onions and bell
pepper in oil until tender. Stir in
remaining ingredients except fish.
Bring to a boil; reduce heat. Cover
and simmer 20 minutes. Add fish.
Simmer 10 to 15 minutes longer or
until fish flakes easily with fork.
Remove bay leaf before serving.
    Makes 10 servings

Presentation: Serve with thick,
crusty bread sticks.

Pescado Viejo

Paella

Paella

1 tablespoon olive oil
½ pound chicken breast cubes
1 cup uncooked rice*
1 medium onion, chopped
1 clove garlic, minced
1½ cups chicken broth
1 can (8 ounces) stewed tomatoes, chopped, reserving liquid
½ teaspoon paprika
⅛ to ¼ teaspoon ground red pepper
⅛ teaspoon ground saffron
½ pound medium shrimp, peeled and deveined
1 small red pepper, cut into strips
1 small green pepper, cut into strips
½ cup frozen green peas

*If using medium grain rice, use 1¼ cups of broth; if using parboiled rice, use 1¾ cups of broth.

Heat oil in Dutch oven over medium-high heat until hot. Add chicken and stir until browned. Add rice, onion, and garlic. Cook, stirring, until onion is tender and rice is lightly browned. Add broth, tomatoes, tomato liquid, paprika, ground red pepper, and saffron. Bring to a boil; stir. Reduce heat; cover and simmer 10 minutes. Add shrimp, pepper strips, and peas. Cover and simmer 10 minutes or until rice is tender and liquid is absorbed.   *Makes 6 servings*

Favorite recipe from **USA Rice Council**

Cioppino

1½ cups chopped onions
 1 cup chopped celery
 ½ cup chopped green pepper
 1 large garlic clove, crushed
 3 tablespoons olive oil
3½ cups (28-ounce can)
     CONTADINA® Whole Peeled
     Tomatoes and juice
1⅓ cups (two 6-ounce cans)
     CONTADINA® Italian Paste
 ½ teaspoon Italian seasoning
 1 teaspoon salt
 ½ teaspoon pepper
 2 cups water
 1 cup dry red wine
 3 to 3½ pounds mixed seafood:
     clams, oysters, mussels,
     shrimp, white fish, scallops,
     cooked crab, cooked lobster,
     or crawfish

In Dutch oven, sauté onions, celery, green pepper, and garlic in oil until tender. Add tomatoes and juice, Italian paste, Italian seasoning, salt, pepper, water, and wine; break up tomatoes. Heat to boiling. Reduce heat; boil gently, uncovered, 30 minutes.

To prepare seafood: scrub clams, oysters, and mussels under running water. Place in ½-inch boiling water in saucepan. Cover and boil gently just until shells open, about 3 minutes (discard any shellfish that do not open). Set aside. Shell and devein shrimp. Cut fish, scallops, crab, and lobster into bite-size pieces.

Add white fish to tomato mixture; boil gently 5 minutes. Add scallops, shrimp, and crawfish; cook additional 5 minutes. Add lobster, crab, and reserved shellfish. Heat to serving temperature.

Makes 3½ quarts

Shrimp Gumbo

 1 package (16 ounces) frozen cut
     okra
 1 can (16 ounces) stewed
     tomatoes, undrained
 2 cups water
 ½ pound cooked ham or sausage,
     diced
 1 can (8 ounces) tomato sauce
 2 medium onions, sliced
 2 tablespoons oil
 ½ teaspoon crushed red pepper
     flakes
 1 bay leaf
     Salt and pepper
 2 pounds frozen shelled
     deveined shrimp

Combine all ingredients except shrimp in Dutch oven. Bring to a boil over high heat. Reduce heat to low. Simmer, partially covered, 30 minutes. Add shrimp; stir well. Cook, partially covered, stirring occasionally, until shrimp are cooked through, 10 to 15 minutes longer. Remove bay leaf before serving.   *Makes 6 servings*

Pleasing Poultry

These stews and soups are hearty enough to be the main dish of your meal and can be accompanied by a vegetable or fruit salad. A cup of these delicious soups also makes a great complement to a hearty entrée.

Hearty Chicken and Rice Soup

10 cups chicken broth
1 medium onion, chopped
1 cup sliced celery
1 cup sliced carrots
¼ cup snipped parsley
½ teaspoon cracked black pepper
½ teaspoon dried thyme leaves
1 bay leaf
1½ cups chicken cubes (about ¾ pound)
2 cups cooked rice
2 tablespoons lime juice
Lime slices for garnish

Combine broth, onion, celery, carrots, parsley, pepper, thyme, and bay leaf in Dutch oven. Bring to a boil over high heat. Stir once or twice. Reduce heat to low. Simmer, uncovered, 10 to 15 minutes. Add chicken; simmer, uncovered, 5 to 10 minutes or until chicken is cooked. Remove and discard bay leaf. Stir in rice and lime juice just before serving. Garnish with lime slices. *Makes 8 servings*

Favorite recipe from **USA Rice Council**

Quick Arroz con Pollo
(Spanish Chicken and Rice)

¾ pound boneless skinless chicken breasts, cut into 1-inch cubes
½ cup chopped onion
1 clove garlic, minced
2 tablespoons vegetable oil
1¾ cups water
1 medium tomato, chopped
One 6-ounce package FARMHOUSE® Savory Chicken Rice Mix
⅓ cup frozen peas, thawed
⅓ cup sliced green pimento-stuffed olives

In large skillet, sauté chicken, onion and garlic in oil 5 to 7 minutes or until chicken is no longer pink. Add water and tomato; bring to a boil. Add Farmhouse® rice and seasoning packet. Reduce heat; cover and simmer 15 minutes. Add peas and olives; cook 5 to 10 minutes longer or until liquid is absorbed. *Makes 4 to 6 servings*

Hearty Chicken and Rice Soup

French Country Chicken Stew

¼ pound sliced bacon, diced
4 boneless, skinless chicken breast halves, cut into 1-inch pieces
1 medium onion, chopped
2 cloves garlic, minced
1 teaspoon dried thyme leaves, crushed
1 can (16 ounces) DEL MONTE® Cut Green Beans or Green Lima Beans, drained
1 can (15 ounces) kidney beans, drained
1 can (14½ ounces) DEL MONTE® Original Recipe Stewed Tomatoes
Salt and pepper to taste

Cook and stir bacon in large skillet over medium-high heat until almost crisp. Add chicken, onion, garlic and thyme. Cook and stir until onion and garlic are soft, about 5 minutes. Pour off drippings.

Add remaining ingredients; bring to a boil over high heat. Reduce heat to low. Simmer, uncovered, 10 minutes.

Makes 4 servings

French Country Chicken Stew

Chicken Marengo

¼ cup olive oil
4 boneless skinless chicken breast halves (about 1 pound), cut into 1-inch cubes
⅓ pound mushrooms, thinly sliced
1 medium onion, thinly sliced
2 cloves garlic, chopped
1 can (28 ounces) crushed tomatoes in tomato purée *or* 4 medium tomatoes, peeled, seeded and quartered*
⅓ cup dry white wine
1 bay leaf
½ teaspoon dried thyme leaves, crushed
½ teaspoon salt
Ground black pepper to taste
½ cup frozen peas
¼ cup sliced pimiento-stuffed green olives
2 tablespoons water
2 tablespoons cornstarch
Boiled red potatoes (optional)
Chopped parsley for garnish

*To peel a tomato, cut a skin-deep "X" in the blossom end. Submerge tomato in saucepan of boiling water 15 seconds. Remove with slotted spoon; plunge immediately into a bowl of cold water 10 seconds. The skin can be pulled off easily with a sharp knife.

Heat oil in 5-quart Dutch oven over medium-high heat. Cook and stir chicken, mushrooms, onion and garlic until onion is soft. Stir in tomatoes, wine, bay leaf, thyme, salt and pepper.

(continued)

Turkey Picadillo

Reduce heat to low. Cover and simmer 20 minutes. Stir in peas and olives; cook 5 minutes more. Discard bay leaf. Blend water with cornstarch in small cup until smooth. Stir into stew. Cook and stir until stew boils and is slightly thickened. Serve with potatoes. Garnish with parsley.   *Makes 4 to 6 servings*

Chicken Vegetable Soup

- 1 **pound boneless skinless chicken breasts, cut into 1-inch pieces**
- 1 **cup chopped onion**
- 2 **cloves garlic, minced**
- 2 **tablespoons FLEISCHMANN'S® Margarine**
- 1 **(10-ounce) package frozen sliced carrots**
- 4 **cups low sodium vegetable juice cocktail**
- 4 **cups water**
- 1½ **cups large bow-tie macaroni**
- 1 **tablespoon Italian seasoning**
- 1 **(10-ounce) package frozen chopped spinach**
- 60 **HARVEST CRISPS® 5-Grain Crackers**

In large saucepan, over medium-high heat, cook chicken, onion and garlic in margarine until onion is tender. Add carrots, vegetable juice, water, macaroni and Italian seasoning. Heat to a boil. Cover; reduce heat to low. Simmer for 20 minutes. Stir in spinach; cook for 5 minutes more. Serve 1 cup soup with 6 crackers.

Makes 10 servings

Turkey Picadillo

- 1 **pound ground turkey**
- ½ **cup chopped onion**
- ¼ **cup chopped green bell pepper**
- 2 **cloves garlic, minced**
- 1 **can (14½ ounces) stewed tomatoes**
- 1 **cup chopped Granny Smith apple**
- ¼ **cup raisins**
- 2 **tablespoons thinly sliced pimiento-stuffed olives**
- 1 **teaspoon sugar**
- ½ **teaspoon ground cinnamon**
- ½ **teaspoon ground cumin**
- ¼ **teaspoon ground cloves**
  Hot cooked rice (optional)
  Toasted almonds (optional)

Cook and stir turkey, onion, green pepper and garlic in large skillet over medium-high heat until turkey is no longer pink. Stir in tomatoes, apple, raisins, olives, sugar, cinnamon, cumin and cloves. Bring to a boil over high heat. Reduce heat to low. Cover and simmer 15 to 20 minutes. Serve over rice; garnish with toasted almonds.

Makes 4 servings

Favorite recipe from **National Turkey Federation**

Garden Patch Turkey Stew with Dumplings

3 cups cubed cooked SWIFT BUTTERBALL® Turkey (1 pound)
1 medium onion, sliced
2 ribs celery, sliced
2 tablespoons butter or margarine
2 cups coarsely chopped cabbage
1 can (14½ ounces) tomatoes, undrained, cut up
1 can (15 ounces) kidney beans, undrained
2 cans (13¾ ounces *each*) chicken broth
1 cup water
2 tablespoons sugar
1½ teaspoons dried marjoram leaves, crushed
1 teaspoon salt
2 cups buttermilk baking mix
⅔ cup milk

Cook and stir onion and celery in butter in Dutch oven or large saucepan over medium heat until crisp-tender. Add turkey, cabbage, tomatoes, beans, broth, water, sugar, marjoram and salt. Cover; reduce heat to low and simmer 25 minutes or until cabbage is tender. Place baking mix in medium bowl. Stir in milk with fork until soft dough forms. Bring stew to a boil over high heat. Drop dough by spoonfuls into boiling stew to make 12 dumplings. Reduce heat to low. Cover and simmer 15 minutes. Serve in bowls.

Makes 6 to 8 servings (12 cups)

Hearty Rice Soup

1 package LIPTON® Rice & Sauce — Chicken Flavor
2 cups chicken broth
2 cups water
½ cup sliced carrots
½ cup sliced celery
¼ cup sliced green onions
1 tablespoon butter or margarine
½ cup cut-up cooked chicken

In medium saucepan, combine all ingredients except chicken; bring to a boil. Continue boiling over medium heat, stirring occasionally, 10 minutes. Stir in chicken and heat through.

Makes 6 (1-cup) servings

Turkey-Olive Ragoût en Crust

½ pound boneless white or dark turkey meat, cut into 1-inch cubes
1 clove garlic, minced
1 teaspoon vegetable oil
¼ cup (about 10) small whole frozen onions
1 medium red potato, skin on, cut into ½-inch cubes
½ cup reduced-sodium chicken bouillon or turkey broth
½ teaspoon dried parsley flakes
⅛ teaspoon dried thyme leaves
1 small bay leaf
10 frozen snow peas
8 whole, small pitted ripe olives
1 can (4 ounces) refrigerator crescent rolls
½ teaspoon dried dill weed

(continued)

Turkey-Olive Ragoût en Crust

1. Preheat oven to 375°F.

2. Sauté turkey and garlic in oil until no longer pink, 3 to 4 minutes, in medium skillet over medium heat. Remove turkey and garlic; set aside.

3. Add onions to skillet; sauté until lightly browned. Add potato, bouillon, parsley, thyme and bay leaf. Bring mixture to a boil over high heat. Reduce heat to low. Cover and simmer 10 minutes or until potato is fork-tender. Remove bay leaf.

4. Combine turkey and potato mixtures. Fold in snow peas and olives. Divide mixture between 2 (1¾-cup) casseroles.

5. Divide crescent rolls into 2 rectangles; press perforations together to seal. Roll out each rectangle to make dough large enough to cover top of casserole, if necessary. Sprinkle dough with dill weed, pressing lightly into dough. Cut small decorative shape from each dough piece; discard or place on baking sheet and bake in oven with casseroles. Place dough over turkey-vegetable mixture; trim dough to fit. Press dough to edge of casserole to seal. Bake 7 to 8 minutes until pastry is golden brown.   *Makes 2 servings*

Note: Brush top of dough with beaten egg yolk before baking for a more golden crust.

Favorite recipe from **National Turkey Federation**

Red Beans and Rice

Vegetable cooking spray
½ cup chopped onion
½ cup chopped celery
½ cup chopped green pepper
2 cloves garlic, minced
2 cans (15 ounces *each*) red
   beans,* drained
½ pound fully cooked low-fat
   turkey sausage, cut into
   ¼-inch slices
1 can (8 ounces) tomato sauce
1 teaspoon Worcestershire sauce
¼ teaspoon ground red pepper
¼ teaspoon hot pepper sauce
3 cups hot cooked rice
   Hot pepper sauce (optional)

*Substitute your favorite bean for
red beans.

Coat Dutch oven with cooking
spray and place over medium-high
heat until hot. Add onion, celery,
green pepper, and garlic. Cook
2 to 3 minutes. Add beans, sausage,
tomato sauce, Worcestershire sauce,
red pepper, and pepper sauce.
Reduce heat; cover and simmer 15
minutes. Serve beans with rice and
pepper sauce.   *Makes 6 servings*

Favorite recipe from **USA Rice Council**

Pantry Soup

½ cup dry pasta (rotini or
   rotelle), cooked and drained
2 teaspoons olive oil
8 ounces boneless skinless
   chicken, cubed
3½ cups (two 14.5-ounce cans),
   CONTADINA® Pasta Ready
   Tomatoes
¾ cup chicken broth
¾ cup water
1 cup garbanzo beans,
   undrained
1 cup kidney beans, undrained
1 package (16 ounces) frozen
   mixed vegetables
2 teaspoons lemon juice

In 5-quart saucepan with lid, heat
oil; sauté chicken about 3 to 4
minutes or until cooked, stirring
occasionally. Mix in tomatoes,
broth, water, garbanzo and kidney
beans; cover and bring to a boil.
Add mixed vegetables and pasta;
bring to a boil. Reduce heat; cover
and simmer for 3 minutes or until
vegetables are tender. Stir in lemon
juice; serve with condiments, if
desired.

Optional condiments: Grated
Parmesan cheese, chopped fresh
basil or parsley, or croutons.
                Makes 6 to 8 servings

Red Beans and Rice

Country Chicken Stew

6 slices bacon, diced
2 leeks, chopped (white part only) (about ½ pound)
3 shallots, chopped
1 medium carrot, cut into ¼-inch pieces
1½ pounds boneless skinless chicken thighs, cut into 1-inch pieces
1½ pounds boneless skinless chicken breasts, cut into 1-inch pieces
½ pound boneless smoked pork butt, cut into 1-inch pieces
1 Granny Smith apple, cored and diced
2 cups dry white wine or chicken broth
1½ teaspoons herbes de Provence, crushed*
1 teaspoon salt
Pepper to taste
2 bay leaves
2 cans (15 ounces *each*) cannellini beans or Great Northern beans, drained

*Substitute ¼ teaspoon *each* rubbed sage, crushed dried rosemary, thyme, oregano, marjoram and basil leaves for herbes de Provence.

Cook and stir bacon in 5-quart Dutch oven over medium-high heat until crisp. Add leeks, shallots and carrot; cook and stir vegetables until leeks and shallots are soft. Stir in chicken, pork, apple, wine and seasonings. Bring to a boil over high heat. Reduce heat to low. Cover and simmer 30 minutes.

Stir in beans. Cover and simmer 25 to 30 minutes more until chicken and pork are fork-tender and no longer pink in center. Remove bay leaves before serving.

Makes 8 to 10 servings

Chicken Stew à la Morocco

¼ cup olive oil
½ pound eggplant, peeled and cubed
1 large onion, sliced
2 to 3 cloves garlic, chopped
2 tablespoons lemon juice
2 teaspoons ground coriander
1 teaspoon ground turmeric
¼ teaspoon crushed red pepper flakes
5 boneless skinless chicken breast halves (about 1½ pounds)
10 boneless skinless chicken thighs (about 1½ pounds)
1 cup chicken broth
¼ cup golden raisins
½ cup sliced pimiento-stuffed green olives
Peel of 1 lemon, coarsely chopped
Hot cooked couscous or rice (optional)
Chopped mint for garnish

Heat oil in 5-quart Dutch oven over medium-high heat. Cook and stir eggplant, onion and garlic in oil until soft. Stir in lemon juice, seasonings and red pepper flakes; move vegetables to side of pan.

(continued)

Brown chicken, in batches, in Dutch oven 10 minutes. Remove with slotted spoon; reserve chicken. Repeat until all remaining chicken is browned. Return chicken to Dutch oven.

Add broth and raisins. Bring to a boil over high heat. Reduce heat to low. Cover and simmer 25 minutes. Stir in olives and lemon peel. Cover and simmer 25 minutes more or until chicken is fork-tender and no longer pink in center. Serve over couscous. Garnish with mint.

Makes 8 to 10 servings

Speedy Brunswick Stew

8 broiler-fryer chicken thighs, boned, skinned, cut into bite-size pieces
1 teaspoon salt, divided
¼ teaspoon pepper
2 tablespoons vegetable oil
1 onion, cut lengthwise into ¼-inch slices
1 can (28 ounces) tomatoes, undrained, broken up
2¼ cups water, divided
1 package (10 ounces) frozen lima beans
1 package (10 ounces) frozen whole kernel corn
1 tablespoon Worcestershire sauce
2 teaspoons chicken bouillon granules
1 teaspoon sugar
2 tablespoons all-purpose flour
2 tablespoons chopped parsley

Sprinkle ¼ teaspoon salt and pepper over chicken. Heat oil in Dutch oven over medium-high heat. Add chicken and onion; cook and stir about 5 minutes.

Add tomatoes, 2 cups water, beans, corn, Worcestershire, bouillon granules, sugar and remaining ¾ teaspoon salt. Bring to a boil over high heat. Reduce heat to low. Cover and simmer 20 minutes or until chicken and vegetables are fork-tender.

Mix flour and remaining ¼ cup water in small bowl. Stir flour mixture into stew. Cook, stirring, until slightly thickened. Sprinkle with chopped parsley.

Makes 6 to 8 servings

Favorite recipe from **Delmarva Poultry Industry, Inc.**

New England Style Turkey Chowder

2 cups diced cooked SWIFT BUTTERBALL® Turkey (¾ pound)
2 cans (17 ounces *each*) cream-style corn
2½ cups milk
1 cup chicken broth
1 cup diced potato
½ cup finely shredded carrot
½ cup finely chopped onion
1 teaspoon salt
¼ teaspoon ground black pepper

Combine all ingredients in large saucepan. Bring to a boil over high heat; reduce heat to low. Cover and simmer 20 minutes, stirring occasionally.

Makes 6 to 8 servings (9 cups)

Indian Summer Turkey Soup

Indian Summer Turkey Soup

4 cups water
1 envelope LIPTON® Recipe Secrets® Noodle Soup Mix with Real Chicken Broth
½ pound cooked smoked or regular turkey breast, diced
1 small tomato, diced
½ cup 1-inch diagonally cut asparagus
½ cup whole kernel corn
¼ teaspoon fennel seeds, crushed (optional)

In large saucepan, bring water to a boil. Stir in remaining ingredients. Bring to a boil, then simmer, uncovered, stirring occasionally, 5 minutes or until asparagus is tender.   *Makes 6 (1-cup) servings*

MICROWAVE DIRECTIONS: In 2-quart microwave-safe casserole, combine water with fennel. Microwave covered at HIGH (Full Power) 10 minutes or until boiling. Stir in remaining ingredients. Microwave, covered, 7 minutes or until asparagus is tender, stirring once. Let stand, covered, 2 minutes.

Chunky Chicken Noodle Soup with Vegetables

2 envelopes LIPTON® Recipe Secrets® Noodle Soup Mix with Real Chicken Broth
6 cups water
½ small head escarole, torn into pieces (about 2 cups)*
1 large rib celery, sliced
1 small carrot, sliced
¼ cup frozen peas (optional)
1 small clove garlic, finely chopped
½ teaspoon dried thyme leaves
2 whole cloves
1 bay leaf
2 cups cut-up cooked chicken
1 tablespoon finely chopped parsley

*Substitute 2 cups shredded cabbage.

In large saucepan or stockpot, combine noodle soup mix, water, escarole, celery, carrot, peas, garlic, thyme, cloves and bay leaf. Bring to a boil, then simmer, uncovered, stirring occasionally, 15 minutes or until vegetables are tender. Stir in chicken and parsley; heat through. Remove bay leaf.
Makes about 4 (1¾-cup) main-dish or 7 (1-cup) appetizer servings

MICROWAVE DIRECTIONS: In 3-quart microwave-safe casserole, combine as above. Microwave uncovered at HIGH (Full Power), stirring occasionally, 20 minutes or until vegetables are tender. Stir in chicken and parsley; microwave, uncovered, 1 minute or until heated through. Remove bay leaf. Let stand covered 5 minutes.

Turkey Mushroom Stew

1 pound turkey cutlets
3 tablespoons butter or
    margarine
1 small onion, thinly sliced
2 tablespoons minced green
    onions with tops
½ pound mushrooms, sliced
2 to 3 tablespoons flour
1 cup half-and-half or milk
1 teaspoon dried tarragon
    leaves, crushed
1 teaspoon salt
    Pepper to taste
½ cup frozen peas
½ cup sour cream (optional)
    Puff pastry shells (optional)

Place turkey cutlets between two sheets of waxed paper. Lightly pound with flat side of meat mallet to ¼-inch thickness. Cut into 4×1-inch strips; set aside.

Melt butter in 5-quart Dutch oven over medium heat. Cook and stir both types of onion in hot butter until soft. Stir in mushrooms; cook 5 minutes more. Remove vegetables with slotted spoon.

Cook and stir turkey in hot butter in same Dutch oven until almost opaque. Blend flour into half-and-half until smooth; stir into turkey. Add tarragon, salt and pepper. Return cooked vegetables to Dutch oven; stir in peas. Bring to a boil over medium heat. Reduce heat to low. Cover and simmer 15 to 20 minutes until turkey is fork-tender and peas are heated through. Remove from heat. Stir in sour cream just before serving, for a richer flavor. Serve in puff pastry shells.   *Makes 4 servings*

Chicken with Zucchini & Tomatoes

4 broiler-fryer chicken breast
    halves, skinned
2 tablespoons olive oil
1 can (14½ ounces) stewed
    tomatoes
2 small zucchini, cut into
    ¼-inch slices
½ teaspoon Italian seasoning
    Salt and pepper to taste

Place oil in skillet; heat to medium-high temperature. Add chicken; cook, turning, 10 minutes or until brown on both sides. Drain off excess fat. Add tomatoes, zucchini, Italian seasoning, salt and pepper. Reduce heat to medium-low; cover and cook about 20 minutes or until chicken and zucchini are fork-tender.   *Makes 4 servings*

Favorite recipe from **Delmarva Poultry Industry, Inc.**

Chicken with Zucchini & Tomatoes

Chicken Scaparella

2 slices bacon, coarsely chopped
2 tablespoons FILIPPO BERIO®
    Olive Oil
1 large chicken breast, split
½ cup quartered mushrooms
1 small clove garlic, minced
1 cup plus 2 tablespoons chicken
    broth
2 tablespoons red wine vinegar
8 small white onions, peeled
4 small new potatoes, cut into
    halves
½ teaspoon salt
⅛ teaspoon pepper
1 tablespoon all-purpose flour
    Chopped parsley

Cook bacon in skillet. Remove bacon with slotted spoon; set aside. Pour off drippings. Add oil and chicken. Brown well on all sides. Add mushrooms and garlic. Sauté several minutes, stirring occasionally. Add 1 cup broth, vinegar, onions, potatoes, salt and pepper. Cover and simmer 35 minutes until chicken and vegetables are tender.

To thicken sauce, dissolve flour in 2 tablespoons chicken broth. Stir into sauce. Cook, stirring, until thickened and smooth. Garnish with reserved bacon and parsley.

Makes 2 servings

Tortilla Soup

3 corn tortillas, 6- to 7-inch
    diameter
  Vegetable oil
½ cup chopped onion
1 small clove garlic, minced
1 can (14½ ounces) tomatoes,
    undrained
2 cans (13¾ ounces *each*) ready-
    to-serve chicken broth
1 cup shredded cooked chicken
2 teaspoons lime juice
1 small avocado, peeled and
    pitted
2 tablespoons cilantro leaves

Cut tortillas in half, then cut crosswise into ½-inch strips. Pour oil to depth of ½ inch in small skillet. Place over medium-high heat until oil reaches 360°F on deep-frying thermometer. Add tortilla pieces, a few at a time; deep-fry 1 minute or until crisp and lightly browned. Remove with slotted spoon; drain on paper towels.

Heat 2 teaspoons oil in 3-quart pan over medium heat. Add onion and garlic; cook until onion is soft. Coarsely chop tomatoes; add to pan. Add chicken broth. Bring to a boil. Cover; reduce heat and simmer 15 minutes. Add chicken and lime juice. Simmer 5 minutes. Dice avocado. Serve soup in individual bowls. Top with avocado, tortilla strips and cilantro.

Makes 4 servings

Chicken Scaparella

Rick's Good-As-Gold Chili

⅓ cup water
¼ cup instant minced onion
2 teaspoons instant minced garlic
½ cup vegetable oil
1½ pounds skinless boneless
    chicken breasts, cut into
    1-inch pieces
1 can (15 ounces) tomato sauce
¾ cup beer
½ cup chicken broth
2 tablespoons chili powder
2 teaspoons ground cumin
1 teaspoon dried oregano,
    crushed
1 teaspoon soy sauce
1 teaspoon Worcestershire sauce
¾ teaspoon salt
½ teaspoon paprika
½ teaspoon ground red pepper
¼ teaspoon ground turmeric
⅛ teaspoon rubbed sage
⅛ teaspoon dried thyme, crushed
⅛ teaspoon dry mustard

Combine water, onion and garlic in small bowl; let stand 10 minutes to soften. Heat oil in large skillet over medium-high heat until hot. Brown half of chicken in skillet. Remove with slotted spoon; set aside. Repeat with remaining chicken.

Pour off all but 2 tablespoons oil from skillet; heat oil until hot. Add softened onion and garlic; cook and stir about 5 minutes or until golden. Add remaining ingredients and chicken; mix well. Bring to a boil. Reduce heat and simmer, stirring occasionally, 20 minutes or until sauce thickens slightly.

Makes 4½ cups

Favorite recipe from **American Spice Trade Association**

Rick's Good-As-Gold Chili

Sweet 'n' Sour Turkey Meatball Stew

2 pounds ground turkey
¾ cup dry bread crumbs
½ cup chopped onion
⅓ cup chopped water chestnuts
1 clove garlic, minced
1 egg
½ teaspoon salt
½ teaspoon ground ginger
¼ teaspoon ground black pepper
4 tablespoons reduced-sodium soy sauce, divided
2 tablespoons vegetable oil
2 cups water
¼ cup apple cider vinegar
¼ cup sugar
1 can (20 ounces) pineapple chunks in juice, drained and juice reserved
1 medium green bell pepper, cut into ½-inch pieces
1 medium red bell pepper, cut into ½-inch pieces
Peel from 1 lemon, coarsely chopped
2 tablespoons cornstarch
Hot cooked rice (optional)

Combine turkey, bread crumbs, onion, water chestnuts, garlic, egg, salt, ginger, black pepper and 1 tablespoon soy sauce in large bowl; mix well. Shape into meatballs.*

Heat oil in 5-quart Dutch oven over medium heat. Brown meatballs in hot oil. Remove with slotted spoon. Discard fat. Combine water, vinegar, sugar and reserved pineapple juice in Dutch oven. Return meatballs to Dutch oven.

Bring to a boil over high heat. Reduce heat to low. Cover and simmer 20 to 25 minutes. Stir in pineapple, bell peppers and lemon peel. Simmer, uncovered, 5 minutes.

Blend remaining 3 tablespoons soy sauce into cornstarch in small bowl until smooth. Bring meatballs to a boil over medium-high heat; stir in cornstarch mixture. Cook 5 minutes or until mixture thickens, stirring constantly. Serve over rice.

Makes 6 servings

*To quickly shape uniform meatballs, place meat mixture on cutting board; pat evenly into large square, one inch thick. With sharp knife, cut meat into 1-inch squares; shape each square into a ball.

Quick Deli Turkey Soup

1 can (13¾ ounces) ready-to-serve chicken broth
1 can (14½ ounces) stewed tomatoes, undrained
1 small zucchini, cut up (about 1 cup)
¼ teaspoon dried basil leaves
½ pound SWIFT BUTTERBALL® Deli Turkey Breast, cubed
½ cup cooked chili-mac pasta or macaroni

Combine broth, tomatoes with juice, zucchini and basil in large saucepan. Bring to a boil over high heat. Reduce heat to medium; simmer 10 minutes or until zucchini is tender. Stir in turkey and pasta. Continue heating until turkey is hot.

Makes 4 servings

Arizona Turkey Stew

Arizona Turkey Stew

> 5 medium carrots, cut into thick slices
> 1 large onion, cut into ½-inch pieces
> 3 tablespoons olive or vegetable oil
> 1 pound sliced turkey breast, cut into 1-inch strips
> 1 teaspoon LAWRY'S® Garlic Powder with Parsley
> 3 tablespoons all-purpose flour
> 8 small red potatoes, cut into ½-inch cubes
> 1 package (10 ounces) frozen peas, thawed
> 8 ounces sliced fresh mushrooms
> 1 package (1.62 ounces) LAWRY'S® Spices & Seasonings for Chili
> 1 cup beef broth
> 1 can (8 ounces) tomato sauce

In Dutch oven, sauté carrots and onion in oil until tender. Stir in turkey strips and Garlic Powder with Parsley; cook 3 minutes or until turkey is just browned. Stir in flour. Stir in remaining ingredients. Bring mixture to a boil; reduce heat.

Cover; simmer 40 to 45 minutes until potatoes are tender. Let stand 5 minutes before serving.

Makes 8 to 10 servings

Presentation: Perfect with a crisp green salad.

OVEN DIRECTIONS: In large skillet, sauté carrots and onion in oil until tender. Stir in turkey strips and Garlic Powder with Parsley; cook 3 minutes or until turkey is just browned. Stir in flour. Pour mixture into 3-quart casserole dish. Stir in remaining ingredients. Bake, covered, in 450°F. oven 40 to 45 minutes or until potatoes are tender. Let stand 5 minutes before serving.

Down-Home Rice & Bean Soup

> 1 tablespoon butter or margarine
> 1 medium zucchini, thinly sliced
> 1 small onion, finely chopped
> 1 small red pepper, chopped (optional)
> ½ teaspoon LAWRY'S® Garlic Salt
> 4 cups water
> 1 package LIPTON® Rice & Beans — Chicken Flavor
> ½ pound boneless skinless chicken breasts, cut into ½-inch cubes
> Grated Parmesan cheese (optional)

In large saucepan, melt butter and cook zucchini, onion, red pepper and garlic salt 2 minutes or until vegetables are tender. Stir in remaining ingredients except cheese; bring to a boil. Reduce heat

(continued)

and simmer, uncovered, stirring occasionally, 10 minutes or until beans are tender. Serve, if desired, with grated Parmesan cheese.

Makes about 6 (1-cup) servings

Chinese Chicken Stew

- 1 package (1 ounce) dried black Chinese mushrooms
- 1 pound boneless skinless chicken thighs
- 1 teaspoon Chinese five-spice powder
- ¼ to ½ teaspoon crushed red pepper flakes
- 1 tablespoon peanut or vegetable oil
- 1 large onion, coarsely chopped
- 2 cloves garlic, minced
- 1 can (about 14 ounces) chicken broth, divided
- 1 tablespoon cornstarch
- 1 large red bell pepper, cut into ¾-inch pieces
- 1 tablespoon soy sauce
- 2 large green onions, cut into ½-inch pieces
- 1 tablespoon Oriental sesame oil
- 3 cups hot cooked white rice (optional)
- ¼ cup coarsely chopped cilantro (optional)

Place mushrooms in small bowl; cover with warm water. Soak 20 minutes to soften. Drain; squeeze out excess water. Discard stems; slice caps. Cut chicken into 1-inch pieces. Toss chicken with five-spice powder in small bowl. Season as desired with red pepper flakes.

Heat wok or large skillet over medium-high heat. Add peanut oil; heat until hot. Add coated chicken, onion and garlic; stir-fry 2 minutes or until chicken is no longer pink.

Blend ¼ cup broth into cornstarch in cup until smooth. Add remaining broth to wok. Stir red bell pepper, mushrooms and soy sauce into stew. Reduce heat to medium. Cover and simmer 10 minutes.

Stir cornstarch mixture and add to wok. Cook and stir 2 minutes or until sauce boils and thickens. Stir in green onions and sesame oil. Ladle into soup bowls; scoop ½ cup rice into each bowl. Sprinkle with cilantro.

Makes 6 servings (about 5 cups)

Chinese Chicken Stew

Versatile Vegetables

The year-round abundance of fresh and frozen vegetables makes these delectable soups and stews a terrific choice at anytime. For dinner-in-a-hurry, serve with a fruit salad and one of the marvelous quick breads in the following chapter.

Southwest Chili

1 large onion, chopped
1 tablespoon olive oil
2 large tomatoes, chopped
1 (4-ounce) can chopped green chilies, undrained
1 tablespoon chili powder
1 teaspoon ground cumin
1 (15-ounce) can red kidney beans, undrained
1 (15-ounce) can Great Northern beans, undrained
¼ cup cilantro leaves, chopped (optional)

Cook and stir onion in oil in large saucepan over medium heat until onion is soft. Stir in tomatoes, chilies, chili powder and cumin. Bring to a boil. Add beans with liquid. Reduce heat to low. Cover and simmer 15 minutes, stirring occasionally. Sprinkle individual servings with cilantro.

Makes 4 servings

Minestrone Soup

2 (13¾-fluid ounce) cans COLLEGE INN® Beef or Chicken Broth
¼ cup uncooked shell macaroni
1 (16-ounce) can mixed vegetables, undrained
1 (16-ounce) can stewed tomatoes, undrained and coarsely chopped
1 (15-ounce) can red kidney beans, drained
1 teaspoon garlic powder
1 teaspoon dried basil leaves

In large saucepan, over medium-high heat, heat all ingredients to a boil. Reduce heat; simmer 20 minutes or until macaroni is cooked.

Makes 6 servings

Top: Southwest Chili
Bottom: Cheesy Corn Sticks (page 79)

Lentil and Brown Rice Soup

Lentil and Brown Rice Soup

- 1 envelope LIPTON® Recipe Secrets® Onion Recipe Soup Mix*
- 4 cups water
- ¾ cup lentils, rinsed and drained
- ½ cup uncooked brown or regular rice
- 1 can (14½ ounces) whole peeled tomatoes, undrained and coarsely chopped
- 1 medium carrot, coarsely chopped
- 1 large stalk celery, coarsely chopped
- ½ teaspoon dried basil leaves
- ½ teaspoon dried oregano leaves
- ¼ teaspoon dried thyme leaves (optional)
- 1 tablespoon finely chopped fresh parsley
- 1 tablespoon apple cider vinegar
- ¼ teaspoon pepper

*Also terrific with Lipton® Recipe Secrets® Beefy Onion or Beefy Mushroom Recipe Soup Mix.

In large saucepan or stockpot, combine onion recipe soup mix, water, lentils, uncooked rice, tomatoes with liquid, carrot, celery, basil, oregano and thyme. Bring to a boil, then simmer covered, stirring occasionally, 45 minutes or until lentils and rice are tender. Stir in remaining ingredients.

Makes about 3 (2-cup) servings

Ratatouille

¼ cup olive or vegetable oil
2 cups chopped onions
2 cloves garlic, minced
4 to 5 cups (1 pound) cubed
    eggplant
1 can (14½ ounces) whole peeled
    tomatoes, undrained,
    chopped *or* 3 tomatoes,
    peeled, chopped
2 cups sliced mushrooms (about
    ⅓ pound)
½ pound zucchini, cut lengthwise
    into halves and sliced (about
    1¼ cups) *or* 1 package
    (10 ounces) frozen sliced
    zucchini
1 green bell pepper, cut into
    strips
1 teaspoon dried basil leaves,
    crushed
1 teaspoon dried oregano leaves,
    crushed
¼ teaspoon salt
    Ground black pepper to taste

Heat oil in 5-quart Dutch oven over medium-high heat. Cook and stir onions and garlic in oil until onions are soft. Stir in eggplant, tomatoes, mushrooms, zucchini, bell pepper, basil, oregano, salt and pepper. Bring to a boil over high heat. Reduce heat to low. Cover and simmer 20 to 25 minutes until vegetables are fork-tender. Cook, uncovered, 5 to 10 minutes more, stirring occasionally, until mixture is slightly thickened.

Makes 4 (1½-cup) servings

Golden Carrot Soup

3 tablespoons margarine
4 tablespoons unsalted butter
3½ cups shredded carrots, in all
1 cup grated onion
1 tablespoon CHEF PAUL
    PRUDHOMME'S MAGIC
    SEASONING BLENDS
    VEGETABLE MAGIC®, in all
3 cups chicken stock or water,
    in all
1 quart heavy cream, in all
¼ teaspoon salt

In 5-quart saucepan over medium-high heat, melt margarine and butter. When they come to a hard sizzle, add 3 cups carrots, onion and 2 teaspoons Vegetable Magic®; stir well. Cook, stirring and scraping frequently, about 20 minutes. Let mixture stick slightly, but not brown.

Stir in 2 cups stock; scrape bottom and side of pan until clean. Cook about 5 minutes, stirring occasionally. Pour in remaining 1 cup stock; cook, stirring occasionally, about 5 minutes more or until mixture comes to a rolling boil.

Whisk in 2 cups cream; cook, whisking occasionally, about 7 minutes. Stir in remaining carrots, cream, Vegetable Magic and salt. Cook 16 to 17 minutes, whisking occasionally, until soup has thickened enough to coat a spoon.

Allow soup to set 10 to 15 minutes before serving for flavors to blend.

Makes about 6 cups

Basil-Vegetable Soup

1 package (9 ounces) frozen cut green beans
1 can (15 ounces) cannellini or Great Northern beans, undrained
3 medium carrots, thinly sliced
3 medium zucchini or yellow squash, cut into thin slices
2 quarts beef broth
2 cloves garlic, minced
   Salt and pepper to taste
2 to 3 ounces uncooked vermicelli or spaghetti
½ cup tightly packed fresh basil leaves, finely chopped
   Grated Romano cheese

Combine vegetables, broth and garlic in Dutch oven. Bring to a boil over high heat. Reduce heat to low. Cover; simmer until carrots are tender. Season with salt and pepper. Add vermicelli; bring to a boil over high heat. Reduce heat to low. Simmer until pasta is tender, yet firm. (Pasta may be cooked separately; add to soup just before serving.) Add basil; simmer until basil is tender. Sprinkle with cheese.
Makes 10 to 12 servings

Basil-Vegetable Soup

Spicy Zucchini-Pepper Stew

2 tablespoons olive oil
1 large onion, chopped
3 cloves garlic, chopped
1 to 2 teaspoons minced seeded jalapeño pepper*
2 jars (12 ounces *each*) roasted red peppers, drained
2 large tomatoes, diced
2 cups thin zucchini slices
   Grated peel of 1 lemon
1 teaspoon dried oregano leaves, crushed
1 teaspoon dried thyme leaves, crushed
½ teaspoon salt
¼ to ½ teaspoon saffron, crushed
   Ground black pepper to taste
2½ cups chicken broth or water
2 tablespoons water
3 tablespoons cornstarch
   Hot cooked rice

*Wear rubber gloves when working with hot peppers; wash your hands in warm soapy water. Avoid touching your face or eyes.

Heat oil in 5-quart Dutch oven over medium-high heat. Cook and stir onion, garlic and jalapeño until onion is soft. Add red peppers, tomatoes, zucchini, lemon peel, oregano, thyme, salt, saffron and black pepper. Cook and stir 5 minutes more; add broth. Bring to a boil over high heat. Reduce heat to low. Cover and simmer 35 minutes.

Blend water into cornstarch in small cup until smooth. Stir into stew. Cook and stir until stew boils and sauce is slightly thickened. Serve over rice.   *Makes 4 to 6 servings*

Easy Tomato Minestrone

    3 slices bacon, diced
    ½ cup chopped onion
    1 large garlic clove, pressed
    3½ cups water
    2⅔ cups (two 10½-ounce cans)
        beef broth, *undiluted*
    2 cups (15-ounce can) Great
        Northern beans, *undrained*
    ⅔ cup (6-ounce can)
        CONTADINA® Tomato Paste
    ¼ cup chopped parsley
    1 teaspoon dried oregano leaves,
        crushed
    1 teaspoon dried basil leaves,
        crushed
    ¼ teaspoon pepper
    ½ cup dry pasta shells, macaroni,
        or vermicelli, broken into
        1-inch pieces
    1 package (16 ounces) frozen
        mixed Italian vegetables
    ½ cup grated Parmesan cheese
        (optional)

In large saucepan, sauté bacon, onion, and garlic until onion is translucent. Stir in water, broth, beans and liquid, tomato paste, parsley, oregano, basil, pepper, and pasta; heat to boiling. Reduce heat; simmer for 15 minutes. Mix in vegetables; cook additional 10 minutes. Serve with Parmesan cheese, if desired.

Makes about 8 servings

Picante Onion Soup

Picante Onion Soup

    3 cups thinly sliced onions
    1 clove garlic, minced
    ¼ cup butter or margarine
    2 cups tomato juice
    1 can (10½ ounces) condensed
        beef broth
    1 soup can water
    ½ cup PACE® Picante Sauce
    1 cup unseasoned croutons
        (optional)
    1 cup (4 ounces) shredded
        Monterey Jack cheese
        (optional)
        Additional PACE® Picante
        Sauce

Cook onions and garlic in butter in 3-quart saucepan over medium-low heat about 20 minutes, stirring frequently, until onions are tender and golden brown. Stir in tomato juice, broth, water and ½ cup picante sauce; bring to a boil over high heat. Reduce heat to low. Simmer, uncovered, 20 minutes. Ladle soup into bowls and sprinkle with croutons and cheese. Serve with additional picante sauce.

Makes 6 servings

Aztec Corn Soup

2 packages (10 ounces each)
  frozen whole kernel corn
3½ cups chicken broth
¼ teaspoon salt
1 large tomato, peeled and
  seeded
¼ cup coarsely chopped onion
½ teaspoon dried oregano leaves,
  crushed
2 tablespoons butter or
  margarine
½ cup heavy cream
  Green pepper strips (optional)

Combine corn, broth and salt in
3-quart saucepan. Bring to a boil
over high heat. Reduce heat to low.
Cover and simmer 4 to 5 minutes
until corn is tender. Remove ½ cup
corn from saucepan with slotted
spoon; set aside. Process remaining
soup until smooth, half at a time, in
blender. Return soup to saucepan.

Process tomato, onion and oregano
in blender until smooth. Heat butter
over medium heat until hot; add
tomato mixture. Cook and stir 4 to
5 minutes or until thickened.

Add tomato mixture to corn mixture
in saucepan; bring to a boil over
high heat. Reduce heat to low;
simmer uncovered, 5 minutes.

Remove soup from heat; gradually
stir in cream. Heat over very low
heat 30 seconds or just until hot. *Do
not boil.* Ladle into bowls. Garnish
with reserved corn and green
pepper.   *Makes 4 to 6 servings*

Southwest Vegetable Chili

1 cup coarsely chopped onions
1 medium green bell pepper, cut
  into ½-inch pieces
2 cloves garlic, minced
½ cup water
2 beef bouillon cubes
1 tablespoon chili powder
½ teaspoon cumin
¼ cup HEINZ® Wine Vinegar
1 can (15 ounces) kidney beans,
  undrained
1 can (14½ ounces) tomatoes,
  undrained and cut into
  bite-size pieces
1 can (11 ounces) whole kernel
  corn, drained
  Hot cooked rice

In 3-quart saucepan, combine
onions, bell pepper, garlic, water,
bouillon, chili powder and cumin;
simmer, covered, 5 minutes or until
vegetables are tender. Stir in
vinegar, beans, tomatoes and corn.
Bring mixture to a boil; simmer,
uncovered, 30 minutes, stirring
occasionally. To serve, spoon
vegetable chili into individual bowls
and top with rice.

Makes 4 servings

Aztec Corn Soup

Creamy Tomato Bisque

½ cup chopped onion
½ cup chopped celery
 1 large crushed garlic clove
 3 tablespoons butter
¼ cup all-purpose flour
¾ teaspoon basil leaves
½ teaspoon marjoram leaves
½ teaspoon salt
⅛ teaspoon white pepper
3½ cups (28-ounce can)
       CONTADINA® Whole Peeled
       Tomatoes and juice
1¼ cups (10.5-ounce can) chicken
       broth
¾ cup water
 1 cup milk, divided

Sauté onion, celery, and garlic in butter in medium saucepan. Stir in flour and seasonings. Cut up tomatoes; stir in tomatoes and juice, chicken broth, and water. Heat to boiling. Reduce heat and boil gently, uncovered, 30 minutes. Pour half of tomato mixture and half of milk into blender container. Process until blended. Repeat with remaining soup and milk. Serve warm or cold.
Makes 6½ cups

MICROWAVE DIRECTIONS:
Combine onion, celery, garlic, and butter in 2-quart microwave-safe casserole. Cover loosely. Microwave on HIGH (100%) power for 5 minutes. Mix in flour and seasonings. Cut up tomatoes; stir in tomatoes and juice, chicken broth, and water. Cover again and microwave on HIGH (100%) power for 15 minutes, stirring halfway through cooking time. Process in blender as above.

Easy Curried Corn Chowder

 1 can (16 ounces) California
       cling peach slices in juice or
       extra light syrup
½ pound bacon, cut into 1-inch
       pieces
 1 onion, thinly sliced
¼ cup all-purpose flour
 2 teaspoons curry powder
½ cup *each* chopped celery,
       sweet red and green bell
       peppers
 1 package (10.5 ounces) frozen
       corn kernels, thawed
 1 large potato, cut into 1-inch
       cubes
 2 cans (13¾ ounces *each*)
       chicken broth
 1 bay leaf
 1 cup half-and-half

Drain peaches; cut slices in half and set aside. Cook bacon until brown in large saucepan over medium heat; remove from pan and drain on paper towels. Reserve. Drain drippings from pan reserving 2 tablespoons. Cook onion in reserved drippings about 8 minutes or until golden brown.

Stir in flour, curry powder, celery and peppers; cook 1 minute. Stir in corn, potato, broth and bay leaf. Bring to a boil, stirring occasionally. Cover and simmer 20 minutes or until potato is tender. Remove from heat. Remove bay leaf; stir in half-and-half and reserved peaches. Ladle soup into serving bowls. Top with reserved crisp bacon just before serving. *Makes 6 servings*

Favorite recipe from **Canned Fruit Promotion Service, Inc.**

Four Bean Chili Stew

2 tablespoons vegetable oil
1 large onion, coarsely chopped
3 cloves garlic, chopped
1 medium zucchini, halved
    lengthwise then thinly sliced
    (about 1 cup)
½ red bell pepper, cut into cubes
1 can (15 ounces) red kidney
    beans, rinsed and drained
1 can (15 ounces) black beans,
    rinsed and drained
1 can (15 ounces) garbanzo
    beans, rinsed and drained
1 can (15 ounces) Great
    Northern beans, rinsed and
    drained
2 cans (11 ounces *each*)
    tomatillos,* drained
1 can (15 ounces) tomato sauce
½ cup barbecue sauce
1½ teaspoons ground cumin
1 to 1½ teaspoons chili powder
½ teaspoon salt
¼ to ½ teaspoon ground red
    pepper
    Sour cream, chopped tomato,
    chopped onion or shredded
    Cheddar cheese for toppings
    Flour tortillas, warmed
    (optional)
    Chopped cilantro for garnish

*Tomatillos are a Mexican green tomato and can be found in Mexican grocery stores or in the specialty food section in large supermarkets.

Heat oil in 5-quart Dutch oven over medium-high heat. Cook and stir onion and garlic in hot oil until onion is soft. Stir in zucchini and bell pepper; cook and stir 5 minutes.

Add all four beans, tomatillos, tomato sauce, barbecue sauce, cumin, chili powder, salt and ground red pepper. Bring to a boil over high heat. Reduce heat to low. Cover and simmer 30 minutes. Serve with desired toppings and tortillas. Garnish with cilantro.

Makes 4 to 6 servings

Brown Rice and Lentil Stew

¾ cup uncooked brown rice
½ cup dry lentils, rinsed
½ cup chopped onion
½ cup sliced celery
½ cup sliced carrots
¼ cup chopped parsley
1 teaspoon Italian herb
    seasonings
1 clove garlic, minced
1 bay leaf
2½ cups chicken broth
2 cups water
1 can (14½ ounces) tomatoes,
    chopped, undrained
1 tablespoon cider vinegar

Combine rice, lentils, onion, celery, carrots, parsley, seasonings, garlic, bay leaf, broth, water, tomatoes and vinegar in Dutch oven. Bring to a boil over high heat. Reduce heat to low. Simmer, uncovered, about 1 hour or until rice is tender, stirring occasionally. Remove bay leaf before serving.   *Makes 4 servings*

Favorite recipe from **USA Rice Council**

Tomato Soup

    1 tablespoon vegetable oil
    1 cup chopped onion
    2 cloves garlic, coarsely chopped
    ½ cup chopped carrot
    ¼ cup chopped celery
    2 cans (28 ounces *each*) crushed
       tomatoes in tomato purée
3½ cups chicken broth*
    1 tablespoon Worcestershire
       sauce
    ½ to 1 teaspoon salt
    ½ teaspoon dried thyme leaves
    ¼ to ½ teaspoon black pepper
    2 to 4 drops hot pepper sauce

*Substitute 2 cans (10½ ounces *each*) condensed chicken broth and 1 cup water for 3½ cups chicken broth.

Heat oil in large Dutch oven over medium-high heat. Add onion and garlic; cook and stir 1 to 2 minutes until onion is soft. Add carrot and celery; cook 7 to 9 minutes until tender, stirring frequently. Stir in tomatoes, broth, Worcestershire sauce, salt, thyme, pepper and hot pepper sauce. Reduce heat to low. Cover and simmer 20 minutes, stirring frequently.

For a smoother soup: Remove from heat. Let cool about 10 minutes. Process soup, in food processor or blender, in small batches until smooth. Return soup to Dutch oven; simmer 3 to 5 minutes until heated through.   *Makes 6 servings*

Corn Chowder Olé

    ½ pound sweet Italian sausage,
       casing removed
    2 (13¾-fluid ounce) cans
       COLLEGE INN® Chicken
       Broth
    1 (16-ounce) jar ORTEGA®
       Medium Thick and Chunky
       Salsa
    ½ teaspoon ground cumin
    1 medium zucchini, sliced
    1 (16-ounce) package frozen
       corn
    1 cup drained kidney beans
    2 cups broken tortilla chips
       Dairy sour cream

In saucepan, over medium-high heat, brown sausage, stirring occasionally to break up meat; remove from pan and set aside. Pour off drippings.

In same pan, over high heat, heat chicken broth, salsa and cumin to a boil; reduce heat to low. Add zucchini; simmer for 10 minutes. Stir in corn, kidney beans and reserved sausage. Simmer 10 minutes more. To serve, portion ¼ cup chips into individual serving bowls. Ladle soup into each bowl; top with dollop of sour cream. Serve immediately.   *Makes 8 servings*

Mexican Tortilla Soup

Mexican Tortilla Soup

6 to 8 corn tortillas (6-inch diameter), preferably day-old
2 large, very ripe tomatoes, peeled, seeded (about 1 pound)
⅔ cup coarsely chopped onion
1 large clove garlic
Vegetable oil
7 cups chicken broth
4 sprigs cilantro
3 sprigs fresh mint (optional)
½ to 1 teaspoon salt
5 ounces Monterey Jack cheese, cut into ½-inch cubes
¼ cup coarsely chopped cilantro

Stack tortillas; cut stack into ½-inch-wide strips. Set aside.

Process tomatoes, onion and garlic in blender until smooth. Heat 3 tablespoons oil in large saucepan over medium heat until hot. Add tomato mixture; cook 10 minutes, stirring frequently.

Stir in broth and cilantro sprigs; bring to a boil over high heat. Reduce heat to low. Simmer, uncovered, 20 minutes. Add mint and salt; simmer 10 minutes more. Remove and discard cilantro and mint sprigs. Keep soup warm.

Heat ½ inch oil in deep, heavy, large skillet over medium-high heat to 375°F; adjust heat to maintain temperature. Fry half of tortilla strips at a time, in single layer, 1 minute or until crisp, turning strips occasionally. Remove with slotted spoon; drain on paper towels.

Ladle soup into bowls. Let each person add tortilla strips, cheese and chopped cilantro according to taste.   *Makes 4 to 6 servings*

Cream of Artichoke Soup

1 jar (6 ounces) marinated
    artichoke hearts
3 large cloves fresh California
    garlic
½ cup chopped onion
2 tablespoons flour
2 cans (10¾ ounces *each*)
    condensed chicken broth
1 cup half-and-half or milk
    Finely chopped parsley

Drain marinade from artichoke
hearts into 2-quart saucepan. Set
aside artichoke hearts. Crush garlic
with press; add to marinade. Add
onion; cook, covered, over low heat
until onion is soft, about 10 minutes.
Blend in flour. Slowly stir in 1 can
broth. Cook over high heat until
mixture comes to a boil, stirring
constantly. Boil 1 minute or until
mixture thickens.

Process artichoke hearts in blender
or food processor until smooth.
Strain into saucepan. Add
remaining can of broth and half-
and-half. Heat just to serving
temperature; *do not boil.* Sprinkle
each serving with parsley.

Makes 4 (1-cup) servings

Favorite recipe from **Christopher Ranch
Garlic**

Bean Soup Provençal

1½ cups *each* chopped onions and
    celery
1 cup sliced leeks
¼ cup vegetable oil
8 cups water
1 cup sliced carrots
1 turnip, peeled and diced
1 teaspoon salt
¼ teaspoon coarsely ground
    pepper
2 cans (about 16 ounces *each*)
    Idaho Great Northern
    beans,* drained
1 small zucchini, sliced
1 cup sliced fresh or frozen
    chopped spinach
    Pesto Sauce (recipe follows)

*Substitute 3⅓ cups drained,
cooked beans.

Sauté onions, celery and leeks in oil
in large saucepan about 10 minutes
or until onions are soft. Add water,
carrots, turnip, salt and pepper.
Bring to a boil over high heat.
Reduce heat to low. Cover and
simmer 30 minutes or until
vegetables are tender. Add beans,
zucchini and spinach; heat
thoroughly. Add 2 tablespoons
Pesto Sauce to soup; pass remaining
sauce.   *Makes 8 to 10 servings*

PESTO SAUCE: Place ½ cup
chopped parsley, ¼ cup *each* olive
oil and grated Parmesan cheese,
1 to 2 cloves garlic, 1 tablespoon
crushed dried basil and 1 teaspoon
lemon juice in blender or food
processor; process until smooth.

Makes about ⅓ cup

Favorite recipe from **Idaho Bean
Commission**

Busy-Day Breads

Easy and fast to make and bake, the aroma of quick breads baking in the oven calls everyone to the kitchen. These freshly baked breads complete a meal, whether it's soup, stew or another entrée.

Garden Vegetable Muffins

2 cups all-purpose flour
2 tablespoons sugar
1 tablespoon baking powder
¼ teaspooon salt
1 package (3 ounces) cream cheese
¾ cup milk
½ cup finely shredded or grated carrots
¼ cup chopped green onions
¼ cup vegetable oil
1 egg

Preheat oven to 400°F. Grease or paper-line 12 (2½-inch) muffin cups.

Combine flour, sugar, baking powder and salt in large bowl. Cut in cream cheese with pastry blender until coarse crumbs form.

Combine milk, carrots, green onions, oil and egg in small bowl until blended. Stir into flour mixture just until moistened. Spoon evenly into prepared muffin cups.

Bake 25 to 30 minutes until golden brown and wooden pick inserted in center comes out clean.

Immediately remove from pan. Cool on wire rack for about 10 minutes. Serve warm.

Makes 12 muffins

Country Recipe Biscuits

2 cups all-purpose flour
1 tablespoon baking powder
½ cup prepared HIDDEN VALLEY RANCH® Original Ranch® Salad Dressing
½ cup buttermilk

Preheat oven to 425°F. In small bowl, sift together flour and baking powder. Make a well in flour mixture; add salad dressing and buttermilk. Stir with fork until dough forms a ball. Drop by rounded spoonfuls onto ungreased baking sheet. Bake until lightly browned, 12 to 15 minutes.

Makes 12 biscuits

Garden Vegetable Muffins

Cheddar Pepper Muffins

2 cups all-purpose flour
1 tablespoon sugar
1 tablespoon baking powder
1 teaspoon coarsely ground
 black pepper
½ teaspoon salt
1¼ cups milk
¼ cup vegetable oil
1 egg
1 cup (4 ounces) shredded sharp
 Cheddar cheese, divided

Preheat oven to 400°F. Generously grease or paper-line 12 (2½-inch) muffin cups. Combine flour, sugar, baking powder, pepper and salt in large bowl. Combine milk, oil and egg until blended in small bowl. Stir into flour mixture just until moistened. Fold in ¾ cup cheese. Spoon into muffin cups. Sprinkle remaining cheese over tops. Bake 15 to 20 minutes until light golden brown. Cool in pan on wire rack 5 minutes. Remove from pan; serve warm. *Makes 12 muffins*

Cheddar Pepper Muffins

Corn Bread

¼ CRISCO® Stick or ¼ cup
   CRISCO all-vegetable
   shortening
¼ cup sugar
2 egg whites
1 cup all-purpose flour
1 cup yellow cornmeal
4 teaspoons baking powder
½ teaspoon salt (optional)
1¼ cups skim milk

Heat oven to 425°F. Grease 9-inch square pan.

Cream shortening and sugar with fork in medium bowl until blended. Add egg whites. Beat until fairly smooth.

Combine flour, cornmeal, baking powder and salt (if used) in separate bowl. Add to shortening mixture alternately with milk. Stir until dry ingredients are just moistened. Pour into prepared pan.

Bake at 425°F for 20 minutes or until light golden brown around edges. Cut into squares. Serve warm.   *Makes 9 servings*

Cheese Scones

1½ cups all-purpose flour
1½ cups uncooked quick-cooking
   oats
¼ cup packed brown sugar
1 tablespoon baking powder
1 teaspoon cream of tartar
½ teaspoon salt
½ cup (2 ounces) finely shredded
   Cheddar cheese
⅔ cup butter, melted
⅓ cup milk
1 egg

Preheat oven to 425°F. Stir together flour, oats, sugar, baking powder, cream of tartar and salt in large bowl. Stir in cheese. Beat together butter, milk and egg in small bowl. Add to dry ingredients, stirring just until mixed. Shape dough into ball; pat onto lightly floured surface to form 8-inch circle. Cut into 8 to 12 wedges. Bake on buttered baking sheet 12 to 15 minutes until light golden brown.

Makes 8 to 12 scones

Favorite recipe from **Wisconsin Milk Marketing Board**

Dilled Popovers

1 cup skim milk
¾ cup EGG BEATERS® Real Egg
   Product
3 tablespoons FLEISCHMANN'S®
   Sweet Unsalted Margarine,
   melted
¾ cup all-purpose flour
¼ cup CREAM OF RICE® Hot
   Cereal
1 teaspoon dried dill weed
½ teaspoon onion powder

In medium bowl, beat milk, Egg Beaters® and margarine until blended.

In small bowl, combine flour, cereal, dill and onion powder; beat into egg mixture until well blended. Pour into 8 well-greased 6-ounce custard cups. Bake at 450°F for 15 minutes; *reduce heat to 350°F.* Bake for 5 to 10 minutes or until puffed and lightly browned. Carefully slit tops of popovers; bake 5 minutes more. Serve immediately.

Makes 8 popovers

Mushroom Crescent Rolls

Mushroom Crescent Rolls

3 tablespoons butter
1 medium-size onion, finely chopped
½ pound mushrooms, finely chopped
¼ cup sour cream
2 tablespoons all-purpose flour
½ teaspoon salt
½ teaspoon pepper
¼ teaspoon dried thyme leaves
2 cans (8-ounces *each*) refrigerated crescent dinner rolls

Preheat oven to 350°F. Melt butter in medium-size saucepan. Add onion; cook over medium heat until onion is soft. Add mushrooms; cook 3 minutes. Remove from heat; stir in sour cream, flour, salt, pepper and thyme. Separate crescent rolls into 16 triangles. Spread mushroom mixture evenly over triangles. Roll up according to package directions. Bake 15 to 20 minutes until golden brown. *Makes 16 rolls*

Favorite recipe from **Pennsylvania Fresh Mushroom Program**

Carrot Quick Bread

1½ cups finely shredded carrots
¾ cup packed brown sugar
¼ cup granulated sugar
1 tablespoon vegetable oil
1 teaspoon baking soda
1 cup boiling water
2 eggs, lightly beaten
1⅓ cups all-purpose flour
1 cup whole-wheat flour
2½ teaspoons baking powder
1 teaspoon salt
⅛ teaspoon ground nutmeg
1 cup chopped walnuts

Preheat oven to 350°F. Combine carrots, sugars, oil and baking soda in large bowl; mix well. Gradually add boiling water; set aside to cool. Add eggs to cooled mixture; mix well. Combine flours, baking powder, salt and nutmeg in medium bowl; mix well. Stir into carrot mixture. Stir in walnuts. Pour batter into greased 9×5-inch loaf pan; let stand 5 minutes. Bake 50 to 60 minutes until wooden pick inserted in center comes out clean. Remove from pan; cool on wire rack. Wrap in foil or plastic wrap; let stand at room temperature overnight before slicing. *Makes 1 loaf*

Biscuit-Onion Wedges

2½ cups biscuit mix
¾ cup milk
2 eggs, divided
1 cup finely chopped onion
⅔ cup dairy sour cream
1 teaspoon LAWRY'S® Seasoned Salt
¼ teaspoon LAWRY'S® Garlic Powder with Parsley
1½ cups (6 ounces) grated Cheddar cheese, divided
½ teaspoon hot pepper sauce

In medium bowl, combine biscuit mix, milk and 1 egg. In separate bowl, beat together remaining egg, onion, sour cream, Seasoned Salt and Garlic Powder with Parsley; stir in 1 cup Cheddar cheese and hot pepper sauce. Stir into batter. Pour into a greased 8-inch round or square baking dish. Bake on center rack in 400°F oven 20 minutes. Sprinkle top with remaining ½ cup cheese; bake 5 to 7 minutes longer or until toothpick inserted in center comes out clean and cheese is melted. Let stand 2 minutes before serving.   *Makes 6 servings*

Presentation: Cut into squares or wedges. Serve warm with margarine.

Hint: Batter can also be used to make muffins or drop biscuits.

Oatmeal Drop Biscuits

1½ cups all-purpose flour
½ cup uncooked quick-cooking oats
1 tablespoon baking powder
2 teaspoons sugar
½ teaspoon salt
½ teaspoon grated orange peel
6 tablespoons butter or margarine
¾ cup milk

Preheat oven to 450°F. Combine flour, oats, baking powder, sugar, salt and orange peel in large bowl. Cut in butter with pastry blender until mixture resembles coarse crumbs.

Stir milk into flour mixture until well mixed. Drop by rounded tablespoonfuls, 2 inches apart, onto ungreased baking sheets.

Bake 10 to 12 minutes until golden brown on bottoms. Serve immediately.
      Makes about 16 biscuits

Oatmeal Drop Biscuits

Caraway Cheese Muffins

1¼ cups all-purpose flour
½ cup rye flour
2 tablespoons sugar
2½ teaspoons baking powder
½ teaspoon salt
1 cup (4 ounces) shredded sharp Cheddar or Swiss cheese
1½ teaspoons caraway seeds
1 cup milk
¼ cup vegetable oil
1 egg

Preheat oven to 400°F. Grease or paper-line 12 (2½-inch) muffin cups.

Combine flours, sugar, baking powder and salt in large bowl. Add cheese and caraway seeds; toss to coat.

Combine milk, oil and egg in small bowl until blended. Stir into flour mixture just until combined. Spoon evenly into prepared muffin cups.

Bake 20 to 25 minutes until golden brown and wooden pick inserted in center comes out clean. Immediately remove from pan. Cool on wire rack about 10 minutes. Serve warm.   *Makes 12 muffins*

Tex-Mex Corn Bread

1 cup yellow cornmeal
¼ cup all-purpose flour
1 teaspoon baking powder
½ teaspoon baking soda
½ teaspoon salt
2 eggs
¾ cup milk
¼ cup vegetable oil
1 can (17 ounces) cream-style corn
¼ cup minced onion
1½ cups (6 ounces) shredded Cheddar cheese
1 can (4 ounces) diced green chilies, drained

Preheat oven to 400°F. Grease 9-inch square pan. Combine cornmeal, flour, baking powder, baking soda and salt in large bowl. Beat eggs, milk and oil until blended in medium bowl. Stir in corn and onion. Pour liquid mixture into dry ingredients; stir just until moistened.

Spoon half of batter into prepared pan. Sprinkle with half of cheese and half of chilies. Cover with remaining batter; top with remaining cheese and chilies. Bake 30 to 35 minutes until a wooden pick inserted in center comes out clean. Cut into squares; serve hot.
Makes 9 to 12 servings

Caraway Cheese Muffins

Spiced Brown Bread Muffins

    2 cups whole-wheat flour
    ⅔ cup all-purpose flour
    ⅔ cup packed brown sugar
    2 teaspoons baking soda
    1 teaspoon pumpkin pie spice
    2 cups buttermilk
    ¾ cup raisins

Preheat oven to 350°F. Grease 6 (4-inch) muffin cups. Combine flours, sugar, baking soda and pumpkin pie spice in large bowl. Stir in buttermilk just until flour mixture is moistened. Fold in raisins. Spoon into muffin cups. Bake 35 to 40 minutes or until wooden pick inserted in center comes out clean. Remove from pan.

Makes 6 giant muffins

Spiced Brown Bread Muffin

Zucchini Basil Muffins

    1½ cups NABISCO® 100% Bran
    1¼ cups skim milk
    ⅓ cup FLEISCHMANN'S® Margarine, melted
    ¼ cup EGG BEATERS® Real Egg Product
    1¼ cups all-purpose flour
    2 tablespoons sugar
    2 teaspoons baking powder
    1 teaspoon dried basil leaves
    ½ cup grated zucchini

Mix bran, milk, margarine and Egg Beaters®; let stand 5 minutes.

In bowl, blend flour, sugar, baking powder and basil; stir in bran mixture just until blended. Stir in zucchini. Spoon into 12 greased 2½-inch muffin-pan cups. Bake at 400°F for 20 to 25 minutes or until done. Serve warm.

Makes 12 muffins

Zucchini Muffins

    1¼ cups skim milk
    ⅓ cup FLEISCHMANN'S® Margarine, melted
    ¼ cup EGG BEATERS® Real Egg Product
    1½ cups NABISCO® 100% Bran With Oat Bran
    1¼ cups all-purpose flour
    ¼ cup firmly packed light brown sugar
    2 teaspoons baking powder
    1 teaspoon ground cinnamon
    ¼ teaspoon ground nutmeg
    ½ cup grated zucchini
    ½ cup seedless raisins

(continued)

In small bowl, combine milk, margarine and Egg Beaters®. Stir in bran; let stand 5 minutes.

In large bowl, combine flour, sugar, baking powder, cinnamon and nutmeg; stir in bran mixture, zucchini and raisins just until blended. Spoon into 12 greased 2½-inch muffin-pan cups. Bake at 400°F for 20 to 25 minutes or until done. Serve warm.

Makes 12 muffins

Cheesy Corn Sticks

½ cup all-purpose flour
½ cup cornmeal
2 teaspoons baking powder
¼ teaspoon salt
½ cup milk
1 egg, beaten
3 tablespoons vegetable oil
½ cup (2 ounces) shredded
   Cheddar cheese

Preheat oven to 425°F. Heat cast-iron corn stick pan in oven while preparing batter.

Combine flour, cornmeal, baking powder and salt in medium bowl; set aside. Combine milk, egg and oil. Add to dry ingredients, stirring just until moistened.

Carefully brush hot pan with additional oil. Spoon batter into prepared pan. Sprinkle batter with cheese. Bake 10 minutes or until lightly browned.

Makes 7 to 9 corn sticks

Sour Cream Biscuits

1¼ cups all-purpose flour
1½ teaspoons baking powder
½ teaspoon salt
¼ teaspoon baking soda
½ cup sour cream
¼ cup light cream or milk

In mixing bowl, stir together flour, baking powder, salt and baking soda. In small bowl, combine sour cream and light cream. Make a well in center of dry ingredients; add sour cream mixture. Stir just until dough clings together and forms a ball.

Knead dough gently on lightly floured surface 10 to 12 strokes. Roll or pat to ½-inch thickness. Cut dough into 2¼-inch rounds.

Using metal spatula, carefully transfer cut biscuits to lightly greased baking sheet. Bake in 375°F oven about 15 minutes or until golden. Serve warm.

Makes 8 biscuits

Favorite recipe from **The Kingsford Products Company**

Quick Garlic-Onion Ring

- ¼ **cup finely chopped green onions**
- 1 **tablespoon butter or margarine, melted**
- 2 **cloves garlic, minced**
- 1 **package (10 biscuit size) refrigerated regular or buttermilk flaky biscuits**

Preheat oven to 400°F. Combine onions, butter and garlic in small bowl; set aside.

Separate dough into individual biscuits. Gently pull apart each biscuit to separate into two halves, making 20 pieces.

Brush one side of each piece with garlic-onion mixture. Arrange pieces, onion-side up and overlapping, in 9-inch circle on ungreased baking sheet.

Bake 10 to 12 minutes until golden brown.

Makes 1 ring or 10 servings

Easy Wonton Chips

- 1 **tablespoon soy sauce**
- 2 **teaspoons vegetable oil**
- ½ **teaspoon sugar**
- ¼ **teaspoon garlic salt**
- 12 **wonton wrappers**

Preheat oven to 375°F. Combine soy sauce, oil, sugar and garlic salt in small bowl; mix well.

Cut each wonton wrapper diagonally in half. Place wonton wrappers on 15×10-inch jelly-roll pan coated with nonstick cooking spray. Brush soy sauce mixture lightly but evenly over both sides of each wonton wrapper.

Bake 4 to 6 minutes or until crisp and lightly browned, turning after 3 minutes. Transfer to cooling rack; cool completely.

Makes 2 dozen chips

Tomato Cheese Bread

- 2 **cups buttermilk baking mix**
- 2 **teaspoons dried oregano leaves, crushed, divided**
- 1¾ **cups (14½-ounce can) CONTADINA® Recipe Ready Tomatoes,* drained, juice reserved**
- ¾ **cup (3 ounces) shredded Cheddar cheese**
- ¾ **cup (3 ounces) shredded Monterey Jack cheese**

*Substitute 1 can (14½ ounces) Contadina® Whole Peeled Tomatoes, chopped, drained, and juice reserved, in place of Contadina® Recipe Ready Tomatoes.

In medium bowl, combine baking mix, 1 teaspoon oregano, and ⅔ cup reserved tomato juice. In 11×7×2-inch greased baking dish, evenly press dough to edge of dish. Sprinkle Cheddar cheese and remaining oregano over batter. Evenly distribute tomato pieces over cheese; sprinkle with Jack cheese. Bake in preheated 375°F oven for 25 minutes, or until edges are golden brown and cheese is bubbly. Cool 5 minutes before cutting into squares to serve.

Makes 12 servings

Pumpernickel Muffins

Pumpernickel Muffins

 1 cup all-purpose flour
½ cup rye flour
½ cup whole-wheat flour
 2 teaspoons caraway seeds
 1 teaspoon baking soda
½ teaspoon salt
 1 cup buttermilk
¼ cup vegetable oil
¼ cup light molasses
 1 egg
 1 square (1 ounce) unsweetened chocolate, melted and cooled

Preheat oven to 400°F. Grease or paper-line 12 (2½-inch) muffin cups.

Combine flours, caraway seeds, baking soda and salt in large bowl.

Combine buttermilk, oil, molasses and egg in small bowl until blended. Stir in melted chocolate. Stir into flour mixture just until moistened. Spoon evenly into prepared muffin cups.

Bake 20 to 25 minutes or until wooden pick inserted in center comes out clean. Immediately remove from pan. Cool on wire rack about 10 minutes. Serve warm or cold. Store at room temperature in tightly covered container up to 2 days.   *Makes 12 muffins*

Jalapeño-Bacon Corn Bread

4 slices bacon
¼ cup minced green onions with tops
2 jalapeño peppers, stemmed, seeded and minced*
1 cup yellow cornmeal
1 cup all-purpose flour
2½ teaspoons baking powder
½ teaspoon baking soda
½ teaspoon salt
1 egg
¾ cup plain yogurt
¾ cup milk
¼ cup butter or margarine, melted
½ cup (2 ounces) shredded Cheddar cheese

*Wear rubber gloves when working with hot peppers; wash your hands in warm soapy water. Avoid touching your face or eyes.

Preheat oven to 400°F. Cook bacon in skillet until crisp; drain on paper towels. Pour 2 tablespoons bacon drippings into 9-inch square baking pan *or* 9-inch cast-iron skillet. Crumble bacon into small bowl; add green onions and peppers.

Combine cornmeal, flour, baking powder, baking soda and salt in large bowl. Beat egg slightly in medium bowl; add yogurt and whisk until smooth. Whisk in milk and butter. Pour liquid mixture into dry ingredients; stir just until moistened. Stir in bacon mixture. Pour into pan; sprinkle with cheese.

Bake 20 to 25 minutes or until a wooden pick inserted in center comes out clean. Cut into squares or wedges; serve hot.
Makes 9 to 12 servings

Raisin Oat Scones

2 cups all-purpose flour
2 teaspoons baking powder
½ teaspoon baking soda
¼ teaspoon salt
1 cup rolled oats
½ cup butter or margarine, chilled, cut into pieces
1 cup raisins
About 1 cup buttermilk

Preheat oven to 425°F. Grease baking sheet.

Sift flour, baking powder, baking soda and salt into medium bowl. Stir in oats. Using pastry blender or 2 knives, cut in butter until mixture resembles coarse crumbs. Add raisins. Stir in enough buttermilk to make soft dough.

Turn out dough onto well-floured surface. Knead dough 10 times. (To knead dough, fold dough in half toward you and press dough away from you with heels of hands. Give dough a quarter turn and continue folding, pushing and turning.) Roll out dough into 12×10-inch rectangle. Cut into 2-inch squares.

Arrange scones on prepared baking sheet. Bake about 15 minutes or until browned.   *Makes 30 scones*

Top: Jalapeño-Bacon Corn Bread
Bottom: Tex-Mex Corn Bread (page 76)

Pumpkin-Ginger Scones

½ cup sugar, divided
2 cups all-purpose flour
2 teaspoons baking powder
1 teaspoon ground cinnamon
½ teaspoon baking soda
½ teaspoon salt
5 tablespoons butter or
    margarine, divided
1 egg
½ cup canned pumpkin
¼ cup sour cream
½ teaspoon grated fresh ginger *or*
    2 tablespoons finely chopped
    crystallized ginger

Preheat oven to 425°F. Reserve 1 tablespoon sugar. Combine remaining sugar, flour, baking powder, cinnamon, baking soda and salt in large bowl. Cut in 4 tablespoons butter with pastry blender until mixture resembles coarse crumbs.

Beat egg in small bowl. Add pumpkin, sour cream and ginger; beat until well combined. Add pumpkin mixture to flour mixture; stir until mixture forms soft dough that leaves side of bowl.

Turn out dough onto well-floured surface. Knead dough 10 times. (To knead dough, fold dough in half toward you and press dough away from you with heels of hands. Give dough a quarter turn and continue folding, pushing and turning.) Roll out dough into 9×6-inch rectangle.

Cut dough into six (3-inch) squares. Cut each square diagonally in half, making 12 triangles. Place triangles, 2 inches apart, on ungreased baking sheets. Melt remaining tablespoon butter. Brush triangles with butter; sprinkle with reserved sugar.

Bake 10 to 12 minutes or until golden brown. Serve immediately.
Makes 12 scones

Dilly Cheese Muffins

2 cups all-purpose flour
1 tablespoon sugar
1 tablespoon baking powder
2 teaspoons dried dill weed
1 teaspoon onion powder
½ teaspoon salt
¼ teaspoon freshly ground black
    pepper
1 cup creamed small curd
    cottage cheese
¾ cup milk
¼ cup margarine or butter,
    melted
1 egg, beaten

Preheat oven to 400°F. Grease or paper-line 12 (2½-inch) muffin cups. Combine flour, sugar, baking powder, dill weed, onion powder, salt and pepper in large bowl. Combine cottage cheese, milk, margarine and egg until blended in small bowl. Stir into flour mixture just until moistened. Spoon into muffin cups. Bake 20 to 25 minutes or until golden and wooden toothpick inserted in center comes out clean. Remove from pan.
Makes 12 muffins

Whole-Wheat Onion Soda Bread

2½ **cups whole-wheat flour**
1½ **cups all-purpose flour**
  3 **tablespoons sugar**
  2 **teaspoons baking powder**
  1 **teaspoon baking soda**
  ½ **teaspoon salt**
  6 **tablespoons butter or margarine**
  1 **egg**
1⅓ **cups buttermilk**
  ½ **cup finely chopped green onions**

Preheat oven to 375°F. Grease 1½-quart round casserole. Combine flours, sugar, baking powder, baking soda and salt in large bowl. Cut in butter with pastry blender until mixture resembles coarse crumbs.

Beat egg in medium bowl. Add buttermilk and onions; beat until well combined. Stir buttermilk mixture into flour mixture until mixture forms soft dough that leaves side of bowl.

Turn out dough onto well-floured surface. Knead dough 12 times. (To knead dough, fold dough in half toward you and press dough away from you with heels of hands. Give dough a quarter turn and continue folding, pushing and turning.) Shape into ball; place in prepared casserole. Cut 4-inch cross, ½ inch deep, in center of dough ball.

Bake 55 minutes or until loaf is golden brown and toothpick inserted in center comes out clean.

Cool bread in casserole on wire rack 10 minutes. Remove bread; cool on rack 30 minutes for easier slicing if serving warm. Or, cool bread completely on rack. Store leftover bread up to 5 days in refrigerator.

Makes 1 loaf or 12 servings

Tip: For a shiny loaf, stir together 1 tablespoon sugar and 2 teaspoons water in small bowl until sugar is dissolved. Brush mixture on top of bread immediately after bread is removed from oven.

Cheesy Lahvosh

12 **small lahvosh (3 inches in diameter)**
  3 **tablespoons butter, melted**
  ¼ **cup grated Parmesan cheese**

Preheat oven to 375°F. Brush lahvosh with butter. Sprinkle with cheese. Place on ungreased baking sheet. Bake 5 minutes or until cheese begins to melt.

Makes 4 servings

Cheesy Lahvosh

Wheat Germ Scones

Wheat Germ Scones

½ cup wheat germ, divided
1½ cups all-purpose flour
2 tablespoons packed brown
  sugar
1 tablespoon baking powder
½ teaspoon salt
6 tablespoons butter or
  margarine
⅓ cup golden raisins, coarsely
  chopped
2 eggs
¼ cup milk

Preheat oven to 425°F. Reserve 1 tablespoon wheat germ. Combine remaining wheat germ, flour, sugar, baking powder and salt in large bowl. Cut in butter with pastry blender until mixture resembles coarse crumbs. Stir in raisins.

Beat eggs in small bowl. Add milk; beat until well mixed. Reserve 2 tablespoons milk mixture. Add remaining milk mixture to flour mixture; stir until mixture forms soft dough that leaves side of bowl.

Turn out dough onto well-floured surface. Knead dough 10 times. (To knead dough, fold dough in half toward you and press dough away from you with heels of hands. Give dough a quarter turn and continue folding, pushing and turning.) Roll out dough into 9×6-inch rectangle.

Cut dough into six (3-inch) squares. Cut each square diagonally in half, making 12 triangles. Place triangles, 2 inches apart, on ungreased baking sheets. Brush triangles with reserved milk mixture; sprinkle with reserved wheat germ.

Bake 10 to 12 minutes or until golden brown. Serve immediately.
Makes 12 scones

Sesame Tortilla Crackers

2 tablespoons olive oil
1 tablespoon sesame seeds
¼ teaspoon onion powder
6 flour tortillas (6 inches in
  diameter)

Preheat oven to 450°F. Combine olive oil, sesame seeds and onion powder in small bowl. Brush oil mixture on one side of each tortilla, stacking tortillas oil-side up.

Cut tortilla stack into 6 wedges using sharp knife. Arrange wedges, oil-side up, in single layer on ungreased baking sheets.

Bake 6 to 8 minutes until crackers are golden brown. Remove crackers from sheets; cool completely on wire racks. Store crackers in airtight container up to 3 days.
Makes 36 crackers

Pepperoni-Oregano Focaccia

1 tablespoon cornmeal
1 package (10 ounces) refrigerated pizza crust dough
½ cup finely chopped pepperoni (3 to 3½ ounces)
1½ teaspoons finely chopped fresh oregano leaves *or* ½ teaspoon dried oregano leaves, crushed
2 teaspoons olive oil

Preheat oven to 425°F. Grease large baking sheet, then sprinkle sheet with cornmeal; set aside.

Unroll dough onto lightly floured surface. Pat dough into 12×9-inch rectangle. Sprinkle half the pepperoni and half the oregano over one side of dough. Fold over dough making 6×4½-inch rectangle.

Roll dough into 12×9-inch rectangle. Place on prepared baking sheet. Prick dough with fork at 2-inch intervals, about 30 times. Brush with oil; sprinkle with remaining pepperoni and oregano.

Bake 12 to 15 minutes or until golden brown. (Prick dough several more times if dough puffs as it bakes.) Cut into squares.
Makes 12 servings

Buttermilk Herb Muffins

2 cups NABISCO® 100% Bran
1¼ cups buttermilk
¼ cup FLEISCHMANN'S® Margarine, melted
¼ cup EGG BEATERS® Real Egg Product
1 cup all-purpose flour
2 tablespoons sugar
1 tablespoon DAVIS® Baking Powder
1 teaspoon dried dill weed

Mix bran, buttermilk, margarine and Egg Beaters®; let stand 5 minutes.

In bowl, blend flour, sugar, baking powder and dill; stir in bran mixture just until blended. (Batter will be lumpy.) Spoon batter into 12 greased 2½-inch muffin-pan cups. Bake at 400°F for 18 to 20 minutes or until done. Serve warm.
Makes 1 dozen

MICROWAVE DIRECTIONS:
Prepare muffin batter as above. Spoon batter into 6 paper-lined 2½-inch microwavable muffin-pan cups, ⅔ cup full. Microwave at **HIGH** (100% power) for 1 minute; rotate pan ½ turn. Microwave at **HIGH** for 1 minute more or until toothpick inserted in center of muffin comes out clean. Let stand in pan 1 minute; remove from pan. Repeat 2 more times to make a total of 18 muffins.

Freezer Buttermilk Biscuits

3 cups all-purpose flour
1 tablespoon baking powder
1 tablespoon sugar
1 teaspoon baking soda
½ teaspoon salt
⅔ cup shortening
1 cup buttermilk

Combine flour, baking powder, sugar, baking soda and salt in large bowl. Cut in shortening with pastry blender until mixture resembles coarse crumbs.

Stir buttermilk into flour mixture until mixture forms soft dough that leaves side of bowl.

Turn out dough onto well-floured surface. Knead dough 10 times. (To knead dough, fold dough in half toward you and press dough away from you with heels of hands. Give dough a quarter turn and continue folding, pushing and turning.) Roll out dough into 8-inch square. Cut dough into 16 (2-inch) squares.*

Line baking sheet with plastic wrap. Place squares on lined sheet. Freeze about 3 hours or until firm. Remove frozen squares from sheet; place in freezer container. Freeze up to 1 month.

Preheat oven to 400°F. Place frozen squares, 1½ inches apart, on ungreased baking sheets. Bake 20 to 25 minutes until golden brown. Serve immediately.

Makes 16 biscuits

*To bake biscuits immediately, preheat oven to 450°F. Prepare dough as directed, but do not freeze. Place squares, 1½ inches apart, on ungreased baking sheets. Bake 10 to 12 minutes until golden.

Cheddar Spoonbread

1½ cups water
¾ cup Regular, Instant or Quick CREAM OF WHEAT® Cereal
1 cup shredded reduced-fat Cheddar cheese
½ cup milk
3 eggs, separated
¼ teaspoon ground black pepper

In large saucepan, over high heat, heat water to a boil; slowly sprinkle in cereal, stirring constantly. Return mixture to a boil; reduce heat. Cook and stir until thickened, about 2 to 3 minutes. Remove from heat; stir in cheese until melted, then milk, egg yolks and pepper. In small bowl, with electric mixer at high speed, beat egg whites until stiff peaks form; gently fold egg whites into cheese mixture. Pour into greased 8×8×2-inch baking dish. Bake at 375°F for 30 to 35 minutes or until set and browned. Serve immediately.   *Makes 6 servings*

Freezer Buttermilk Biscuits

Whole-Wheat Flatbreads

1 cup whole-wheat flour
1 tablespoon packed light brown
    sugar
¼ teaspoon salt
¼ cup water
2 tablespoons butter or
    margarine, melted
1 egg white, slightly beaten
1 tablespoon wheat germ or
    sesame seeds

Preheat oven to 375°F. Combine flour, sugar and salt in small bowl. Stir in water and butter until mixture forms a ball.

Knead dough on lightly floured surface about 1 minute until smooth. (To knead dough, fold dough in half toward you and press dough away from you with heels of hands. Give dough a quarter turn and continue folding, pushing and turning.) Divide dough into 4 pieces. Roll out each piece into 7-inch circle. Place circles, 1 inch apart, on ungreased baking sheets. Brush circles lightly with beaten egg white and sprinkle with wheat germ.

Bake 12 to 15 minutes or until edges of flatbreads are browned. Remove flatbreads from baking sheets; cool completely on wire racks. Store flatbreads in airtight container up to 3 days.

Makes 4 (7-inch-round) flatbreads

Bran Crescents

½ cup NABISCO® 100% Bran
½ cup firmly packed light brown
    sugar
¼ cup FLEISCHMANN'S®
    Margarine, melted
1 (8-ounce) package refrigerated
    crescent dinner roll dough

In small bowl, combine bran, brown sugar and margarine. Separate crescent rolls into 8 triangles; sprinkle each triangle with 1 tablespoon bran mixture. Shape crescents and bake as directed on package. Serve warm.

Makes 8 crescents

Spicy Onion Bread

2 tablespoons instant minced
    onion
⅓ cup water
1½ cups biscuit baking mix
1 egg, slightly beaten
½ cup milk
½ teaspoon TABASCO® pepper
    sauce
2 tablespoons butter, melted
½ teaspoon caraway seeds
    (optional)

Preheat oven to 400°F. Soak instant minced onion in water 5 minutes. Combine biscuit mix, egg, milk and TABASCO sauce and stir until blended. Stir in onion. Turn into greased 8-inch pie plate. Brush with melted butter. Sprinkle with caraway seeds. Bake 20 to 25 minutes or until golden brown.

Makes 8 servings

Carrot Muffins

1½ cups NABISCO® 100% Bran
1 cup SUNSWEET® Prune Juice
½ cup shredded carrot
2 egg whites
¼ cup margarine, melted
⅓ cup sugar
1¼ cups all-purpose flour
1 tablespoon baking powder

Mix bran and juice; let stand 5 minutes. Stir in carrot, egg whites, margarine and sugar.

In small bowl, combine flour and baking powder. Stir into bran mixture just until blended. Spoon batter into 12 greased 2½-inch muffin-pan cups.

Bake at 400°F for 15 to 18 minutes or until done. Serve warm.

Makes 1 dozen

Buttermilk Cornbread

2 tablespoons butter or margarine
1½ cups cornmeal
½ cup all-purpose flour
1 tablespoon sugar
2 teaspoons baking powder
½ teaspoon salt
1½ cups buttermilk
½ teaspoon baking soda
2 eggs
4 tablespoons butter, melted
¼ cup chopped jalapeño peppers,* or to taste
1 tablespoon chopped pimiento

*Wear rubber gloves when working with hot peppers; wash your hands in warm soapy water. Avoid touching your face or eyes.

Buttermilk Cornbread

Preheat oven to 425°F. Place 2 tablespoons butter in deep baking dish or quiche pan. Place baking dish in preheated oven just before baking cornbread; heat to melt butter and coat pan.

Sift cornmeal with flour, sugar, baking powder and salt into a large bowl; set aside. Measure 1½ cups buttermilk in large measuring cup; stir in baking soda. Add eggs; beat lightly with a fork. Stir in 4 tablespoons melted butter.

Add buttermilk mixture, peppers and pimiento to cornmeal mixture. Mix until just blended; do not overmix. Pour into heated baking dish. Bake 15 to 20 minutes or until bread is just set. Cut into wedges.

Makes 8 servings

Note: Cornbread should always be served hot. Do not prepare it until you are just about ready to serve dinner.

Acknowledgments

The publisher would like to thank the companies and organizations listed below for the use of their recipes and photographs in this publication.

Alberto Culver Co.

American Lamb Council

American Spice Trade Association

Armour Swift-Eckrich

Canned Fruit Promotion Service, Inc.

Chef Paul Prudhomme's Magic Seasoning Blends®

Christopher Ranch Garlic

Delmarva Poultry Industry, Inc.

Del Monte Corporation

Dole Food Company, Inc.

Farmhouse Foods Company

Filippo Berio Olive Oil

Heinz U.S.A.

The HVR Company

Idaho Bean Commission

The Kingsford Products Company

Lawry's® Foods, Inc.

Thomas J. Lipton Co.

McIlhenny Company

Nabisco, Inc.

National Fisheries Institute

National Live Stock & Meat Board

National Pork Producers Council

National Turkey Federation

Nestlé Food Company

Pace Foods, Ltd.

Pennsylvania Fresh Mushroom Program

The Procter & Gamble Company

StarKist Seafood Company

USA Rice Council

Wisconsin Milk Marketing Board

*I*ndex